Step Forward
Language for Everyday Life

Workbook

SERIES DIRECTOR
Jayme Adelson-Goldstein

3 Janet Podnecky

OXFORD
UNIVERSITY PRESS

OXFORD
UNIVERSITY PRESS

198 Madison Avenue
New York, NY 10016 USA

Great Clarendon Street, Oxford OX2 6DP UK

Oxford University Press is a department of the University of Oxford.
It furthers the University's objective of excellence in research, scholarship,
and education by publishing worldwide in

Oxford New York

Auckland Cape Town Dar es Salaam Hong Kong Karachi
Kuala Lumpur Madrid Melbourne Mexico City Nairobi
New Delhi Shanghai Taipei Toronto

With offices in

Argentina Austria Brazil Chile Czech Republic France Greece
Guatemala Hungary Italy Japan Poland Portugal Singapore
South Korea Switzerland Thailand Turkey Ukraine Vietnam

OXFORD and OXFORD ENGLISH are registered trademarks of
Oxford University Press

Executive Publisher: Janet Aitchison
Editorial Manager: Stephanie Karras
Senior Editor: Sharon Sargent
Art Director: Maj-Britt Hagsted
Art Editor: Justine Eun
Production Manager: Shanta Persaud
Production Controller: Eve Wong

ISBN: 978 0 19 439234 1

Printed in China
15 14 13 12

Illustrations: Shawn Banner: 22, 46; John Batten: 37, 45, 71; Kathy Baxendale: 10,
19, 28, 59; Annie Bissett: 8, 11, 56, 63, 72, 84; Arlene Boehm: 9, 16, 64, 65; Kevin
Brown/Top Dog Studios: 4, 44, 50; Sam Collins: 51; Laurie A. Conley: 2, 15; Bill
Dickson/Contact Jupiter: 9, 61; Jon Keegan: 53; Uldis Klavins: 58, 68.

Photographs: Alamy: Brand X Pictures, 11 (beach); Coston Stock, 39; Jeff
Greenberg, 11 (golf); Jon Arnold Images, 11 (hotel); Profimedia. CZ s.r.o.,
43; Getty Images: Aura/Taxi, 29; Photo Edit, Inc.: Myrleen Ferguson Cate,
48; Michael Newman, 25; Tom Prettyman, 7; James Shaffer, 49; Punchstock:
Bananastock, 11 (restaurant); Purestock, 60.

This book is printed on paper from certified and well managed sources.

I would like to express my deep gratitude to Ashli Totty
for her encouragement and patience throughout this
project. I am also grateful to Meg Brooks and others
on the team at Oxford University Press who offered so
many ideas and suggestions.

I'm especially thankful to my family, Josef and Michelle,
for their support and understanding when the midnight
oil had to be burned.

Janet Podnecky

It's been a privilege to work with Step Forward's gifted
team of editors, designers, and authors. Special thanks
to Janet Podnecky—for her ability to go beyond "fill in
the blank," to Ashli Totty— for her expertise and good
humor, to Sharon Sargent—for her point of view, and to
Jane Spigarelli—for the book without which this book
would not be.

For those who love the phrase, "Open your workbook."

Jayme Adelson-Goldstein

CONTENTS

Learning Together

A Match the pictures with the words.

_1_ take notes	___ make a study schedule	___ organize materials	___ search online
___ make an outline	___ (do) research	___ take a break	___ memorize words

B Match the students with the schools.

_f_ 1. Ivan is 23 years old and studying for the GED.

___ 2. Sara is in sixth grade this year.

___ 3. Oscar just started eleventh grade.

___ 4. Carolina is in first grade.

___ 5. Trinh has his GED and just started a two-year program.

___ 6. Hetal began a four-year engineering program.

a. community college

b. elementary school

c. university

d. middle school

e. high school

f. adult school

A Complete Irina's journal entry. Use the words in the box.

to introduce	a presentation	first assignment	~~first day of~~
was nervous	to meet	talk about	about ourselves

Wednesday, September 12

Today was the _____first day of_____ English class. It was really
                           1

fun. At the beginning of the class, our teacher, Ms. Hampton, asked us

_____ ourselves. I _____,
       2   3

but it was interesting _____ my classmates.
                        4

Then we worked in groups. We had to _____
                                   5

our goals for the class. For our _____, Ms. Hampton
                               6

asked us to write _____. Then she asked us to give
                     7

_____ about what we wrote. We all learned a lot
        8

about each other. I want to do another assignment like this again tomorrow.

B Mark the sentences T (true) or F (false).

__F__ 1. Today was the last day of English class.

____ 2. Ms. Hampton asked the class to introduce themselves.

____ 3. In class, Irina was nervous at first.

____ 4. The students didn't work in groups.

____ 5. Irina had to write about her class.

____ 6. Irina learned a lot in the class.

A **Complete the sentences with the simple present, present continuous, or simple past. Use the information in the chart.**

When?	Kate and Pilar	Marco	Marcella
last week	stay home	finish his class	write an essay
every day	listen to the radio	work	go to the gym
right now	study in the library	play basketball	read a book

1. Kate and Pilar _____stayed home_____ last week.

2. Last week, Marco _____.

3. Every day, Kate and Pilar _____.

4. Last week, Marcella _____.

5. Marco _____ every day.

6. Kate and Pilar _____ right now.

7. Right now, Marco _____.

8. Marcella _____ right now.

B **Write sentences. Use the simple present, present continuous, or simple past.**

1. I / not / study / right now

   I am not studying right now.

2. Alan / take notes / in class / last night

   _____

3. Hana / not / memorize / the new words / last week

   _____

4. We / search / the Internet / every day

   _____

5. They / not / take / notes / right now

   _____

6. Our teacher / help us / a lot / every week.

   _____

C **Match the questions with the answers.**

_b_ 1. Did Tim talk to you?

_____ 2. Does he come to class every week?

_____ 3. Is he studying here now?

_____ 4. Are your friends in the library now?

_____ 5. Do they often go to the movies?

_____ 6. Did they see the new movie?

a. No, they don't.

b. Yes, he did.

c. No, they didn't.

d. Yes, he is.

e. No, they aren't.

f. No, he doesn't.

D **Grammar Boost** **Read the letter. Then rewrite the letter with the correct verb forms.**

Dear Sammy,

Hi! How are you? Everything is OK here. Yesterday, I <u>study</u> for two hours for my English test. I'm glad I did. The test was long, but I think I did well.

Right now, Barbara and Carol <u>watch</u> TV. They <u>learned</u> a lot by watching TV every day.

I <u>liked</u> to use the Internet to find interesting ways to help me study. In our last class, the teacher <u>ask</u> us to bring a newspaper article to the next class. Yesterday, I <u>find</u> an article about good study habits.

<u>Do you go</u> home to visit your family last week? <u>Do you have</u> a good time? I hope so.

Talk to you soon,

Marcos

Dear Sammy,

    Hi! How are you? Everything is OK here. Yesterday, I studied

for two hours for my English test.

_____

_____

_____

_____

_____

_____

_____

_____

_____

    Talk to you soon,

Marcos

A **Complete the conversation. Use the words in the box.**

studying economics	should think about	do you like	~~thinking about~~
so many choices	not sure	worked in	hard to say

David: I'm thinking about a job in computer programming.

Luis: That sounds interesting.

David: What about you? What kind of career are you _____thinking about_____?

1

Luis: There are _____. I'm just _____.

2   3

David: What kinds of things _____ to do?

4

Luis: It's _____. I _____ an office last year,

5   6
and I enjoyed that. I'm _____ right now. I like my class.

                                    7

David: You_____ a career in banking. It's a good field, and there

                            8
are lots of opportunities.

B **Circle the correct words.**

1. I don't always write (clear /(clearly)).

2. We are always (careful / carefully) and check our work.

3. In our group, we answered the questions (quick / quickly).

4. I think she teaches (good / well).

5. The assignment was (easy / easily).

C **Real-life math** **Read the information. Do the math problems. Then label the chart with the correct percentages.**

A survey asked 800 students about their career plans. Here's what they said.

160 students: "I'm planning a career in banking."

1. _160 ÷ 800 = .20 or 20%_

144 students: "I'm planning a career in education."

2. _____

96 students: "I'm planning a career in health care."

3. _____

400 students: "It's hard to say. I'm really not sure."

4. _____

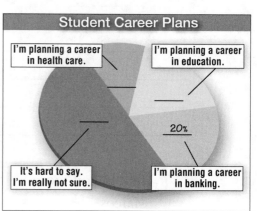

Real-life reading

A **Read the website.**

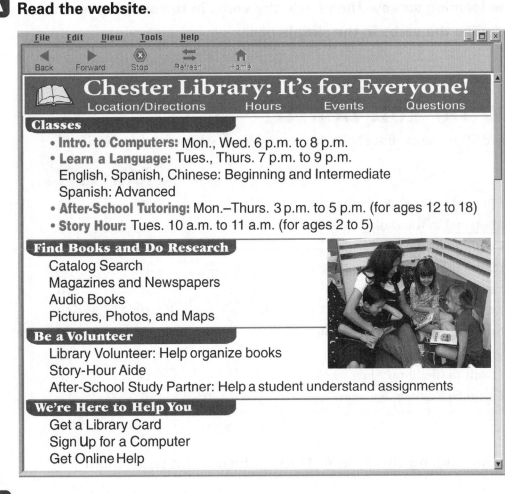

B **Look at A. Circle *a* or *b*.**

1. _____ is a class for children.
   a.) Story Hour
   b. Intro. to Computers

2. After-School Tutoring is for _____.
   a. children ages 2 to 5
   b. children ages 12 to 18

3. To look for a book on computer graphics, go to _____.
   a. Be a Volunteer
   b. Find Books and Do Research

4. To find out the library's hours, go to _____.
   a. Hours
   b. Location/Directions

5. Ana has some free time and likes to help others. She should go to _____.
   a. Be a Volunteer
   b. Find Books and Do Research

6. Carla needs a library card. She should go to _____.
   a. We're Here to Help You
   b. Find Books and Do Research

A **Read the learning survey. Then circle the verbs in the simple present, and underline the verbs in the simple past.**

ESL Student TODAY -

How Do You Learn?

We asked 20 students about how they learn. Here's what they told us:

		Number who say yes	Number who say no
1.	I (listen) to the radio every day.	5	15
2.	I listened to the radio yesterday	8	12
3.	I use the Internet every day.	15	5
4.	I used the Internet yesterday.	16	4
5.	I speak clearly.	4	16
6.	I write carefully.	2	18
7.	I made a clear study schedule.	12	8
8.	I memorize words quickly.	10	10
9.	I went to the library last week.	14	6
10.	I studied English last year.	6	14

B **Look at the learning survey in A. Find 3 adverbs and write them.**

1. _____ 2. _____ 3. _____

C **Write the correct percentages for the students who answered yes.**

1. ___5 ÷ 20 = .25 or 25%___ of the students listen to the radio every day.

2. _____ of the students listened to the radio yesterday.

3. _____ of the students use the Internet every day.

4. _____ of the students used the Internet yesterday.

5. _____ of the students speak clearly.

6. _____ of the students write carefully.

7. _____ of the students made a clear study schedule.

8. _____ of the students memorize words quickly.

9. _____ of the students went to the library last week.

10. _____ of the students studied English last year.

UNIT 2

Ready for Fun

LESSON 1 Vocabulary

A Complete the sentences. Use the words in the box.

farmers' market   ~~amusement park~~   gym   zoo   nightclub   theater

What's Happening this Weekend at Fiesta Village

Fun for all! Over 25 rides for young and old! Lots to see and do at the __amusement park__
1

See all the animals up close at the _____
2

Check out the fresh-picked fruit and vegetables at the
_____
3

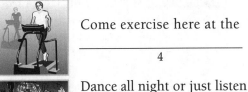
Come exercise here at the
_____
4

Dance all night or just listen to the music at the
_____
5

This weekend is your last chance to see Victor Reyes in the play, *The King Enters*, at the
_____
6

B Match the pictures with the sentences.

__e__ 1. It's loud in this place!

____ 2. I love this show! It's entertaining!

____ 3. It's very relaxing here.

____ 4. This is really boring!

____ 5. Wow! It's exciting!

____ 6. I can't move at all! It's crowded.

A **Look at the pictures. Complete the email. Use the words in the box.**

to a concert	at 5:00	Hi Oscar	~~Sunday evening~~
are you	get together	Think about	Talk to you soon

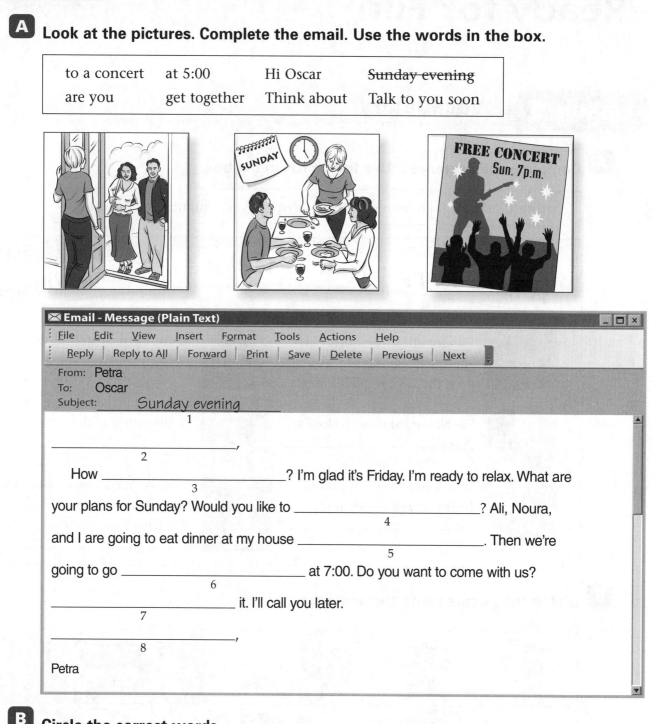

> **✉ Email - Message (Plain Text)**   _ ☐ ✕
>
> File   Edit   View   Insert   Format   Tools   Actions   Help
>
> Reply | Reply to All | Forward | Print | Save | Delete | Previous | Next
>
> From: Petra
> To: Oscar
> Subject: _____Sunday evening_____
>
> _____,
>   2
>
>   How _____? I'm glad it's Friday. I'm ready to relax. What are
>   3
>
> your plans for Sunday? Would you like to _____? Ali, Noura,
>   4
>
> and I are going to eat dinner at my house _____. Then we're
>   5
>
> going to go _____ at 7:00. Do you want to come with us?
>   6
>
> _____ it. I'll call you later.
>   7
>
> _____,
>   8
>
> Petra

B **Circle the correct words.**

1. Petra wrote an email to ((Oscar) / Ali).
2. The subject of the email is (dinner / Sunday evening).
3. They're going to eat at (5:00 / 7:00).
4. They're going to go to (a concert / Petra's house) at 7:00.
5. Petra is going to (call / see) Oscar later.

A Look at the brochure. Write sentences with *be going to* and the words in parentheses.

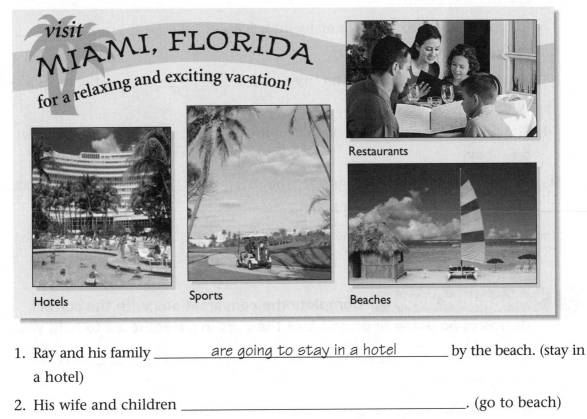

visit
MIAMI, FLORIDA
for a relaxing and exciting vacation!

Restaurants

Hotels

Sports

Beaches

1. Ray and his family _____ are going to stay in a hotel _____ by the beach. (stay in a hotel)

2. His wife and children _____. (go to beach)

3. He _____. (play sports)

4. His children _____. (not sail)

5. His son _____. (swim in the ocean)

6. His daughter _____. (not swim in the ocean)

B Complete the sentences. Use *will* for a promise or prediction. Use *be going to* for a plan.

1. I promise. I _'ll_ call you tonight.

2. Lia has a plan. She _____ take a vacation next month.

3. The newspaper predicts we _____ have a long, hot summer.

4. Don't worry. I _____ give you a ride.

5. Marta _____ stay home and study tonight.

6. We think we _____ have a test next week.

C Complete the predictions. Use *will* and the verbs in parentheses.

1. Many people are moving to the city. The city _____will build_____ more apartments. (build)

2. Computers are important for many jobs. Schools _____ more computer classes. (offer)

3. The roads are falling apart. The city _____ the roads soon. (fix)

4. The price of gasoline is very high. People _____ smaller cars. (buy)

5. People want to spend time outside. The city _____ more parks and recreation areas. (plan)

6. There's a lot of garbage in the river. The city _____ the river. (clean up)

D **Grammar Boost** Complete the conversations with the correct forms of *be going to* or *will*. Use the cues in parentheses to help you.

1. A: What time _____are_____ you _____going to_____ leave for the airport? (plan)

   B: My brother _____ pick me up at 7:00. (promise)

2. A: When _____ you _____ call me? (plan)

   B: I _____ call at 9:00. (promise)

3. A: Where _____ you _____ be after class? (plan)

   B: I don't know. I _____ wait for you at the coffee shop. (promise)

4. A: Who _____ pick up the tickets for the concert? (promise)

   B: Carol _____ get them. She works near the concert hall. (plan)

5. A: _____ Simon and Thomas _____ be at work tomorrow? (plan)

   B: No. They _____ be at a meeting in Boston. (plan)

6. A: When _____ you _____ take me shopping? (plan)

   B: I _____ take you after work. (promise)

A **Complete the conversation. Use the words in the box.**

See you	up to you	do you have in mind
~~Would you like to~~	I'll meet you	I think I'd rather

Sharon: _Would you like to_ _____ get together this weekend?
                               1

Mike: Sure. What _____?
                                  2

Sharon: Well, on Sunday there's a concert or a baseball game.

It's_____.
                       3

Mike: _____ go to the baseball game.
                       4

Sharon: OK. _____ at the stadium at 12:30.
                              5

Mike: That sounds great. _____ then.
                                               6

B **Complete the questions with *would rather*. Then answer the questions. Use your own information.**

1. A: _Would_____ you ___rather____ eat out tonight or make something at home?

   B: _I'd rather eat out._____

2. A: _____ you _____ watch TV or take a walk?

   B: _____

3. A: _____ you _____ go swimming or play tennis?

   B: _____

C **Real-life math** **Read about Sharon and Mike. Answer the questions.**

   Sharon and Mike are going to the baseball game at the stadium. Sharon is bringing her three younger cousins. One cousin is 15 years old. One cousin is 11 years old. Her youngest cousin is five years old. Sharon gives the man at the ticket counter $50 for the tickets for everyone.

Cougars and Giants Baseball Game

SUNDAY: 1:30

TICKETS
Adults: $6.50
Children ages 6–12: $4.50
Children ages 5 and under: free

1. What is the total cost of the tickets? _____

2. How much change will Sharon receive? _____

A Read the article.

The *News of the Day* Entertainment Report: What Our Readers Do for Fun

People today are working more and more and relaxing less and less. It's important to work, but it's also important to have fun and relax. Having fun helps us rest and feel better.

So what do people do for fun? *News of the Day* asked 30 of our readers about their favorite fun activities.

Ten of our 30 readers, or 33%, say they like to read. They read because it's a great activity and they can do it anywhere at any time. All they need is a book, a magazine, or a newspaper. It doesn't take a lot of energy, and they can learn at the same time!

Eight of our 30 readers, or 26%, enjoy spending time with their families. They talk, visit and play with each other.

Our other readers said that they enjoy using the computer, working in the garden, exercising and walking. So when you can, do something fun. Relax. You'll feel better.

Reading	33%
Spending time with the family	26%
Using the computer	20%
Working in the garden	10%
Exercising	7%
Walking	4%

B Mark the sentences T (true) or F (false).

___F___ 1. Today, people spend less time working.

_____ 2. It's important to spend time having fun.

_____ 3. The most popular activity takes a lot of energy.

_____ 4. Thirty percent of readers spend time with family.

_____ 5. Twenty-five percent of readers exercise for fun.

_____ 6. Ten percent of readers work in the garden.

A **Read the conversation. Then underline examples of *will*, and circle examples of *be going to*.**

Ivan: What are you going to do this afternoon?

Tina: We're going to see the new movie at the Town Theater. Do you want to come with us?

Ivan: No, thanks. We saw it last night. I bet you'll love it.

Tina: I think I will. The newspaper says it's a great movie.

Ivan: We're going to have a party for Olga's sister tonight. Why don't you come by after the movie?

Tina: What time?

Ivan: The party is going to start at about 8:00. We'll be in the backyard. Walk around to the back of the house when you get there.

Tina: OK. We'll stop by after the movie.

Ivan: Great. I'll see you tonight.

B **Read the sentences. Check (✓) plan, promise, or prediction.**

	Plan	Promise	Prediction
1. What are you going to do?	✓		
2. We're going to see the new movie at the Town Theater.			
3. You'll love it.			
4. I think I will.			
5. We're going to have a party for Olga's sister tonight.			
6. The party is going to start at about 8:00.			
7. We'll be in the backyard.			
8. We'll stop by after the movie.			
9. I'll see you tonight.			

A Job to Do

A **Look at the ad. Write the answers to the questions.**

1. How much is the digital camera?   It's $149.99.

2. How much is the headset?   _____

3. How much is the keyboard?   _____

4. How much is the CPU?   _____

B **Who says these things? Write the job titles. Use the words in the box.**

| photographer   graphic designer   office manager   ~~computer technician~~ |

1. "I need to fix this CPU and repair the system."   _____computer technician_____

2. "Let me check my camera. OK, now, smile!"   _____

3. "I use my computer and graphics to design pictures."   _____

4. "I keep the office organized and everyone working on schedule."   _____

C **Read the sentences. Match the underlined words with their meanings.**

__b__ 1. My computer <u>crashed</u> again!

a. small area on the computer screen

____ 2. I need to close this <u>window</u>.

b. stopped working

____ 3. There's a new <u>virus</u> in the system.

c. display on the monitor of programs and folders

____ 4. I started my computer but I don't see the <u>desktop</u>.

d. a program that causes computer problems

A Complete the memo. Use the words in the box.

are arriving late	must be at work by	are taking 30-minute	Break times
may not eat or drink	~~Steve Karra~~	are not cleaning their	Employee Policies

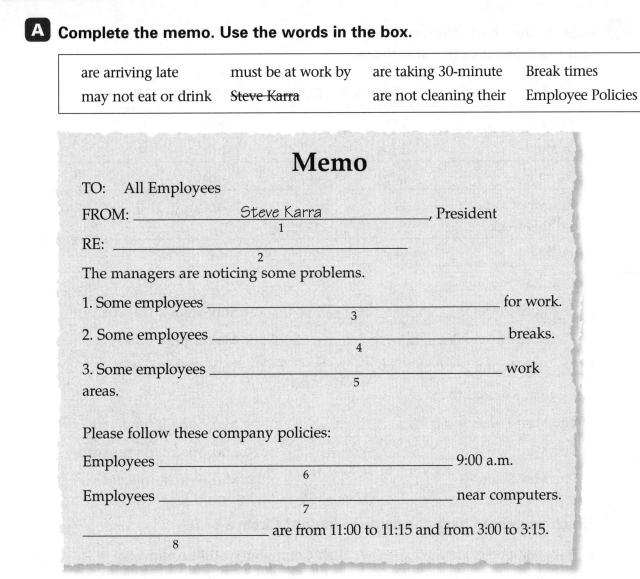

Memo

TO: All Employees

FROM: _____ Steve Karra _____, President
                     1

RE: _____
                     2

The managers are noticing some problems.

1. Some employees _____ for work.
                               3

2. Some employees _____ breaks.
                               4

3. Some employees _____ work
                               5
areas.

Please follow these company policies:

Employees _____ 9:00 a.m.
                          6

Employees _____ near computers.
                          7

_____ are from 11:00 to 11:15 and from 3:00 to 3:15.
          8

B Circle *a* or *b*.

1. The memo is for ____.

   a. All Employees

   b. Steve Karra

2. The memo is from ____.

   a. All Employees

   b. Steve Karra

3. ____ are reporting some problems.

   a. The employees

   b. The managers

4. ____ arrive after 9:30 every day.

   a. Some people

   b. All the workers

5. ____ must clean their work areas.

   a. The managers

   b. The employees

6. There ____ every day.

   a. are two breaks

   b. is one break

A Look at the chart. Then complete the sentences. Use comparative words and the adjectives in parentheses.

	Max-Sound Radio	Mini-Power Radio
Price	$194	$94
Weight	3 lbs.	1 lb.
Size	large	small
Number of radios sold this week	12	20
Reliable	yes	no

(not) as...as

1. The Mini-Power is ___not as expensive as___ the Max-Sound. (expensive)

2. The Mini-Power is _not as heavy as_ the Max-Sound. (heavy)

3. The Max-Sound is _not as small as_ the Mini-Power. (small)

(less...than / more...than)

4. The Mini-Power is _more popular than_ the Max-Sound. (popular)

5. The Mini-Power is _less expensive than_ the Max-Sound. (expensive)

6. The Max-Sound is _reliable than_ the Mini-Power. (reliable)

B Which sentences have the same meaning? Circle *a* or *b*.

1. Hal's computers are less expensive than Computer World's computers.

    a. Hal's computers are as expensive as Computer World's computers.

    (b.) Computer World's computers are more expensive than Hal's computers.

2. Hal's salespeople are not as friendly as Computer World's salespeople.

    (a.) Hal's salespeople are less friendly than Computer World's salespeople.

    b. Hal's salespeople are as friendly as Computer World's salespeople.

3. Computer World is more popular than Hal's.

    a. Hal's is as popular as Computer World.

    (b.) Hal's is less popular than Computer World.

4. Computer World's technicians are not as experienced as Hal's technicians.

    a. Computer World's technicians are more experienced than Hal's technicians.

    (b.) Computer World's technicians are less experienced than Hal's technicians.

C Look at the chart. Write the answers to the questions.

	Trans-Phone $49.99	Express Phone $39.99	Phone Anywhere $24.99
cheap	★	★ ★	★ ★ ★
light	★ ★	★ ★ ★	★
small	★	★ ★	★ ★ ★
popular	★ ★	★ ★ ★	★
reliable	★ ★ ★	★ ★	★

1. Which phone is the cheapest? _Phone Anywhere is the cheapest._
2. Which phone is the lightest? _Express Phone is the lightest_
3. Which phone is the smallest? _Phone anywhere is the smallest_
4. Which phone is the least popular? _Phone anywhere is the least popular_
5. Which phone is the most reliable? _Trans Phone is the most Reliable_
6. Which phone is the most popular? _Express phone is the most popular_

D Grammar Boost — Complete the ad. Circle the correct words.

Cameras R Us
Grand Opening

The (newer / (newest)) Cameras R Us opens this weekend
in Springfield. Our new store is ((larger) / largest) than any other store in
town. Come see our new low prices!

- Our prices are ((lower) / lowest) than the prices at Camera Stop or
Camera Mart. Come see the service!

- Our salespeople are the (friendlier / (friendliest)) salespeople in the city.

- We offer the (faster / (fastest)) and (more complete / (most complete))
service around.

- We are here to help you! Come and see for yourself!

A Complete the conversation. Use the words in the box.

You have to	is it	won't have to tell
most creative person	~~can I see you~~	good worker

Mr. Young: Charles, _____can I see you_____ for a minute?
                                        1

Charles: Yes, Mr. Young. What _____?
                                        2

Mr. Young: You're a _____. You're the _____
                                        3   4
in the office.

Charles: Thanks, Mr. Young.

Mr. Young: But, you take very long breaks. _____ come back
                                        5
from your breaks on time.

Charles: I'm sorry. You _____ me again.
                                        6

Mr. Young: Thank you, Charles.

B Complete the sentences. Use the superlative form of the words in parentheses.

1. Jack is not organized. He's the _____least organized_____ person I know. (organized)

2. San is polite and kind to everybody. He's the _____ person in the office. (nice)

3. Everyone likes Paula. She's the _____ person in the company. (patient)

4. Azim never finishes his work on time. He's the _____ person in the office (efficient)

C **Real-life math**   Read the chart. Write the answers to the questions.

1. What is Maddie's best subject?
   _____Math_____

2. What is her worst subject?
   _____

3. What is her grade point average?
   _____

Name: Maddie Hanel	Grade: 11	
English	B	(3.0)
History	C	(2.0)
Math	A	(4.0)
Science	B	(3.0)
Art	B	(3.0)

A   Read the memo.

Ralston Radio, Inc.
518 Western Boulevard
Houston, TX

MEMO:
To: All staff and employees
From: Maria Wilson, Training Manager
Date: 11/14/07
RE: Learning and Training Classes

Learn more and earn more. Starting January 18, Ralston Radio is providing training classes for all of our employees in the Houston office. Classes are short (four weeks) and small (12 students in each class). We have many great teachers, too, so sign up soon!

Learn the newest technology and the latest skills to help you do a better job and prepare you for a better position at Ralston. Classes include:

- **Management Training:** Do you want to be an office manager?
  Come learn how to keep an office organized and in order. Learn how to make work schedules and supervise others.

- **Design Training:** If you're interested in graphic design, you should take this class. Learn how to make posters and brochures. You can use graphics to design pictures.

- **Computer Technology:** Do you want to be a computer technician? Take this class and learn about new computer programs. Learn how to fix CPUs and repair computer systems.

For more information email me at maria@ralston.us.

B   Mark the sentences T (true), F (false), or NI (no information).

__F__   1. These classes are only for managers.

_____   2. Maria Wilson teaches a class.

_____   3. The classes begin in January.

_____   4. In Design Training, you can learn how to supervise others.

_____   5. You can learn about designing pictures in Management Training.

_____   6. In Computer Technology, you can learn how to fix CPUs.

Look at the pictures. Then write sentences. Use the adjectives in parentheses with *not as...as* and *more...than* or *less...than*.

1. Leo

   (organized)   <u>Leo is not as organized as Rosa and Gloria.</u>

                  <u>He is less organized than Rosa and Gloria.</u>

   (efficient) _____

   _____

   (reliable) _____

   _____

2. Rosa

   (organized)   Rosa is not as organized as Gloria

              She is more organized than Leo

   (efficient) _____

   _____

   (reliable) _____

   _____

3. Gloria

   (organized) _____

   (efficient) _____

   (reliable) _____

Good Work

Vocabulary

A **Look at the notes. Complete the chart.**

Interview with Amy Kim

On time
Cell phone on
Dressed professionally
Forgot resume
Not nervous

Interview with Juan Perea

Ten minutes late
No cell phone
Dressed inappropriately
Good resume
Nervous

	Amy Kim		Juan Perea	
Do's	Yes	No	Yes	No
Arrive on time	✓			✓
Dressed appropriately	✓			✓
Bring resume		✓	✓	
Do not's	Yes	No	Yes	No
Leave cell phone on	✓			✓
Act nervous		✓		✓

B **Who says these things? Match the statements with the type of worker.**

_b_ 1. Everyone says I have great ideas.

_d_ 2. I can fix any problem, big or small.

_f_ 3. I work well with other people.

_a_ 4. I don't need a lot of supervision. I can work on my own.

_c_ 5. I see what needs to be done, and then I do it!

_e_ 6. I'm good at showing people what to do and supervising others.

a. a self-starter

b. a creative thinker

c. a go-getter

d. a problem solver

e. a good leader

f. a team player

A Complete the letter. Use the words in the box.

Sincerely	of accounts manager	learning more about
~~Dear Ms. Sopal~~	organization and communication	555-4114

Ms. Sopal, Personnel Manager
Linwood Communications Corp.
457 West Park Drive
Tampa, FL 33602

Dear Ms. Sopal :
     1

Thank you for the opportunity to interview for the position _of accounts manager_
     2

I enjoyed _learning about_ your company. I hope to have the chance to
     3

use my _orga. and comm._ skills at Linwood Communications.
     4

If you have any questions, or need more information, please call me at

_____. You can also email me at abecker@abc.us.
     5

Sincerly ,
     6

Alberto Becker

Alberto Becker

B Circle *a* or *b*.

1. _____ interviewed Alberto.
   a. Ms. Sopal
   b. Mr. Becker

2. Alberto applied for the _____ position.
   a. personnel manager
   b. accounts manager

3. Alberto has organization and _____ skills.
   a. communication
   b. interview

4. The interviewer can call Alberto at _____.
   a. 555-4114
   b. abecker@abc.us

A Complete the sentences with the present perfect. Use the verbs in parentheses.

1. Don _____has completed_____ high school. (complete)

2. I _have studied_ English since last March. (study)

3. We _have practiced_ interview questions several times. (practice)

4. Bonita _has had_ three interviews in the past few weeks. (have)

5. My brother _hasn't fixed_ the problem with the car. (not fix)

6. Our neighbors _____ here for ten years. (be)

7. Sophie _____ them for two weeks. (not see)

8. They _____ us to their home many times. (invite)

B Complete the sentences with *for* or *since.*

1. Cyrus has worked here _____for_____ three months.

2. He hasn't been in class _____ last week.

3. We've been here _____ 2:00.

4. Has Lucy been at the library _____ two hours?

5. Linda has been my neighbor _____ several years.

6. She has lived here _____ ten years.

7. James and I have been married _____ January.

8. We haven't read the news _____ two days.

C Complete the sentences with the present perfect and *for* or *since*. Use the verbs in parentheses.

1. Li-Anh _____has lived_____ in San Diego _____for_____ three years. (live)

2. She _____ in an office _____ June 2005. (work)

3. She _____ an office manager _____ one year. (be)

4. She _____ English _____ 2001. (not study)

5. Li-Anh _____ any letters _____ May. (not write)

6. She _____ five people _____ 9:00 this morning. (interview)

D Read the sentences. Then circle the correct words.

1. Lisa has fixed computers for three years. She ((fixes) / doesn't fix) computers now.

2. Lisa and Arturo have lived in Chicago. They (live / don't live) in Chicago now.

3. They've lived in California since 2004. They (live / don't live) there now.

4. We've been sick for two days. We (feel / don't feel) sick now.

5. Our friends have visited New York. They (are / aren't) still there.

E 🚀 Grammar Boost Rewrite the sentences. Use the present perfect of the underlined verbs and *for* or *since*.

1. Emma <u>works</u> for the TV station. She started working there eight years ago.

   Emma has worked for the TV station for eight years.

2. Emma and Paul <u>are married</u>. They got married in 2002.

   _____

3. Paul <u>doesn't study</u> English now. He stopped studying last year.

   _____

4. They <u>live</u> in an apartment downtown. They started living there two months ago.

   _____

5. Paul works for Warwick Industries. He started working there in December.

   _____

A **Complete the conversation. Use the words in the box.**

Have you been	I've been	can do it	a good leader
I'm a fast	How long	for four	What makes you think

Ms. Seldon: __How long__ _____ have you been a salesperson at Gibson's?

1

Luis: _____ I've been _____ a salesperson here ___ For four ___

2   3

years.

Ms. Seldon: __What makes you think__ you should be the new sales manager?

4

Luis: I'm __a good leader__. I want to teach other salespeople what

5

I've learned.

Ms. Seldon: __Have you been__ a manager before?

6

Luis: No, but __I'm a fast__ learner, and I know I

7

__Can do it__.

8

Ms. Seldon: That's great, Luis.

B **Underline the contractions. Write the subjects, the full forms of the verbs, and any past participles.**

1. <u>I've</u> finished my work for today. ___I have finished___

2. <u>He's</u> worked at the store since May. __He has__

3. We <u>haven't</u> done the work. __We have not done__

4. <u>She's</u> gotten a new job. __She has gotten__

5. <u>She's</u> been the teacher's assistant for two months. __She has been__

6. The letter <u>hasn't</u> arrived. __It has not arrived__

7. <u>They've</u> had several interviews. __They have had__

8. I <u>haven't</u> talked to the manager. __I have not talked__

C **Real-life math** **Read the paragraph. Then answer the questions.**

The Grand Hotel manager has offered a promotion to Sokanna. The job is Wednesday through Sunday from 2:30 p.m. to 10:30 p.m. The pay will be $21.50 per hour.

1. How much is the gross pay for each day Sokanna works? __$172__

2. How much is the gross pay for every week? __$860__

A Read the article.

How Do I Get That Promotion?

How do you let your supervisor know that you have the skills for that promotion? You need to show your supervisor that you're ready for a promotion. Tell your supervisor what you can do. Most supervisors are looking for people with good communication skills, problem-solving skills, teamwork skills, flexibility, and creativity.

How are your communication skills?

- Are you a good listener?
- Can you give instructions or explain something to another person?

Tell your supervisor about these experiences.

How are you at solving problems?
What do you do when there is a problem?

- Do you study what happened?
- Do you find out what caused the problem?
- Do you try different things to correct the problem?

Tell your supervisor how you solved some problems.

How are you at working with others?

- Do you like working on group projects in a group?
- Do you share your ideas in a group?
- Do you help others in a group?

Talk about groups you have worked with. Give examples of your teamwork skills.

Are you flexible? Creative?

- Do you try new ways to do your work?
- Do you like learning new things at work?
- Do you ever change the way you work?

When you talk to your supervisor, be specific. Talk about what you have done.
Talk about what you can do for the company. Explain why you should get the promotion!

B Mark the sentences T (true), F (false), or NI (no information).

__T__ 1. To get a promotion, tell your supervisor what you can do.

_____ 2. Supervisors don't care about good communication skills.

_____ 3. It's a good idea to study why problems happen.

_____ 4. It's not important to try different things to correct a problem.

_____ 5. You shouldn't share ideas with other employees.

_____ 6. Don't worry about good teamwork skills.

_____ 7. It's important to try different ways to do work.

_____ 8. Flexible employees get promoted 25% of the time.

A Read the article in the company news.

New Business Manager

Congratulations to Nick Sato on his promotion to business manager. Nick <u>has been</u> at Blue Skies Music for eight years. We are pleased that he is now leading the business department.

Al Gonzales, president of Blue Skies, says that Nick has great communication skills. "I've seen Nick do great things at Blue Skies. He listens to people, and he cares about them. He's trained many of our new employees in the basics. He's an excellent person to manage the business department."

One of Nick's new jobs will be to organize a problem-solving team. Nick has done a lot of work with problem solving. Nick said, "I've worked on two very interesting team projects since I started at Blue Skies. We've made some

big changes since then, and I think things are working better now." He also said, "I haven't had time to talk to everyone in the business department, but I hope to talk to all of them soon."

With Nick's skills in problem solving and teamwork, we look forward to great things from the business department.

B Complete the tasks.

1. One example of the present perfect is underlined. Underline six more examples of the present perfect in the article.

2. Find the sentence with *for* and a period of time. Write it here.

   _____

3. Find the 2 sentences with *since* and a time when an activity began. Write them here.

   _____

   _____

4. Find the contractions in the article. Rewrite them using the full forms of the verbs.

   _____   _____

   _____   _____

   _____   _____

Community Resources

LESSON 1 Vocabulary

A Where should I go? Match the sentences with the community resources.

_b_	1. I need to take a job-training class.	a. the animal shelter
____	2. I need low-cost health services.	b. the employment agency
____	3. I need to complete forms for my car.	c. the senior center
____	4. I'm 65 years old, and I want to take a class.	d. the Department of Motor Vehicles
____	5. I need to find city offices.	e. City Hall
____	6. I lost my cat, and I want to find it.	f. the community clinic

B Complete the flyer. Use the words in the box.

volunteer programs	open house	wellness checkup	~~job fair~~	pet adoption

Looking for work? Part-time and full-time positions available.
Come to the
① _job fair_
on **Saturday, June 10**
from **9 a.m to 5 p.m.**

Community Resources

Cats and dogs looking for new homes. Call the Animal Shelter about
④ _____
today!

Every Sunday afternoon, there is an
② _____
at the Senior Center. Come see the services we offer.

Do you have a few hours a week to help others in need? Join one of our
③ _____

Help your children stay healthy.
Call and make an appointment for a
⑤ _____
for them.

A   **Complete the letter. Use the words in the box.**

discussed the problem	~~on behalf of the students~~	invite you to visit
can see the problem	about a safety issue	are broken windows

Board Member Edwin Peterson

New City Schools

212 Learning Way

Detroit, MI 48201

Dear Board Member Peterson,

    I am writing to the school board __on behalf of the students__ in my English class.

                                                        1

We are worried _____.

                          2

    The problem is that there _____ in our classroom. We've

                                                         3

_____ with our school principal, but she says there is no

                 4

money for repairs right now.

    We _____ our school, so you _____.

                         5   6

We hope you can help us make our school safe.

Sincerely,

Chu Pheng

B   **Match the pictures with the problems.**

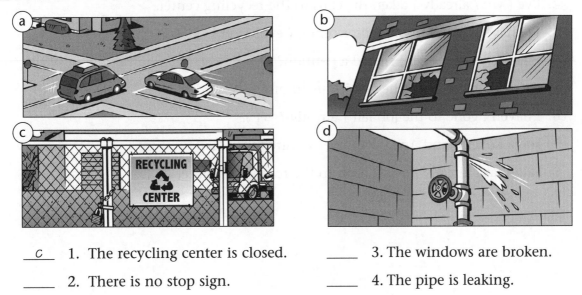

_c_   1. The recycling center is closed.   ____   3. The windows are broken.

____   2. There is no stop sign.   ____   4. The pipe is leaking.

A Write *Yes/No* questions. Use the present perfect.

1. you / fix / the door

   Have you fixed the door?

2. Diana / paint / the apartment

   _____

3. Kevin / repair / the broken windows

   _____

4. Leo and Chan / be / to the animal shelter

   _____

5. you / write / a letter to the school board

   _____

6. they / take / a job-training class

   _____

7. the children / have / a wellness checkup

   _____

8. we / discuss / all the problems

   _____

B Circle the correct words.

1. Have you (ever / yet) done any volunteer work?
2. I've (yet / already) taken the cans to the recycling center.
3. We haven't gone to the senior center (ever / yet).
4. Has Larry (yet / ever) signed a petition?
5. He's (ever / already) helped in his community garden.
6. I haven't gone to the job fair (already / yet).
7. Have Roberto and Ana (ever / yet) visited City Hall?
8. Sally has (already / ever) been to the recreation center.

C **Match the questions with the answers.**

<u> c </u> 1. Have you ever been to New York?   a. No, he'll study French next semester.

_____ 2. Has Don ever studied another   b. No, she hasn't fixed it yet.
       language?

_____ 3. Have Luis and Marcos already   c. Yes, I went there last month.
       signed the petition?

_____ 4. Has Marie already fixed the   d. Yes, he made it an hour ago.
       computer?

_____ 5. Has Mark made dinner yet?   e. Yes, they did that yesterday.

D 🚀 **Grammar Boost**   **Look at the picture. Write the sentences.**

Things Ramiro has done:

1. <u>Ramiro has already mixed the paint.</u>

2. _____

3. _____

Things Ramiro hasn't done:

4. <u>Ramiro hasn't cleaned the floor yet.</u>

5. _____

6. _____

A **Complete the conversation. Use the words in the box.**

sounds like a great	have you signed	~~Did you go~~
so sorry	What's it	We're asking

Rick: Hi, Patty. _____ Did you go _____ to the meeting on Thursday?

1

Patty: No, I didn't, Rick. I'm _____.

2

Rick: That's OK. By the way, _____ the petition yet?

3

Patty: No, I haven't. _____ about?

4

Rick: We need more places to collect bottles, papers, and cans.

_____ the mayor's office for more recycling centers.

5

Patty: More recycling centers? Where do I sign? That _____ idea.

6

B **Circle the correct words.**

1. Have you ever ((been) / was) to a community meeting?

2. Maggie didn't (go / gone) to the meeting yesterday.

3. She has (had / have) a cold for two days.

4. Did Tam (volunteer / volunteered) to help?

5. We haven't (sign / signed) the petition.

C **Real-life math** **Use the graph to complete the sentences.**

1. About 25 percent of the people in Windsor volunteered in _____ 1990 _____.

2. Volunteering did not increase between _____ and 1985.

3. Between 1980 and 2005, volunteering increased by about _____ percent.

Windsor Volunteer Rates, 1980–2005

Percent

50
40
30
20
10
0

1980 1985 1990 1995 2000 2005

A Read the flyer.

Keep Our State Beautiful

This group started in 2001 to protect the environment.

Litter Pickers

organizes volunteers to pick up trash in public places. For information or to volunteer, call 555-9944.

State Parks Program

Help clean up the parks in our state. Last year our volunteers picked up more than 10,000 pounds of trash! You can make a difference. **Call 555-3333 today.**

TRASH

No Pollution Now

Now you can report pollution problems when you see them. If you see litter, water pollution, or other environmental problems, let us know and we'll check it out.[1] **Call us: 555-1000.**

Community Improvement Grants[2]

Does your community need money for an environmental project? If so, Community Improvement Grants may be the answer. We help programs that want to stop littering, protect our natural resources, and make our communities beautiful. Call Paula at 555-2626.

[1] check it out: find out more information about it
[2] grant: a gift of money for a specific use

B Mark the sentences T (true), F (false), or NI (no information).

_F_ 1. Litter Pickers pays people to pick up litter.

____ 2. Last year, volunteers for the State Parks Program picked up over 10,000 pounds of trash.

____ 3. Litter Pickers will pick up trash at your house.

____ 4. Many people volunteer for No Pollution Now.

____ 5. Community Improvement Grants will help programs that want to stop littering.

____ 6. Community Improvement Grants provided over $15,000 to the community last year.

A Read the questionnaire. Then answer the question.

Name: Clara

Have you ever…	YES	NO
1. taken things to a recycling center?	✓	
2. written a letter about a problem?		✓
3. volunteered to clean up trash?	✓	
4. signed a petition?		✓
5. planted trees in your community?	✓	
6. gone to a community meeting?		✓
7. celebrated Earth Day?	✓	
8. reported problems in your community?		✓

If you answered "yes" to questions 1, 3, 5, or 7, you should volunteer for the **Clean Up Now** program.
If you answered "yes" to questions 2, 4, 6, or 8, you should volunteer for the **Make a Difference** program.

Should Clara volunteer for "Clean Up Now"+- or "Make a Difference"?

_____

B Look at A. Write the sentences.

Things Clara has done:

1. Clara has taken things to a recycling center.

2. _____

3. _____

4. _____

Things Clara hasn't done:

5. Clara hasn't written a letter about a problem.

6. _____

7. _____

8. _____

What's Cooking?

LESSON 1   **Vocabulary**

A Match the words with the picture.

__1__ glass	____ boil	____ knife	____ chop	____ plate
____ fork	____ pour	____ stir	____ pot	____ bowl

B Complete the sentences. Use the words in the box.

grater	steamer	slicer	mixer	~~peeler~~	beater

1. I want to peel the potatoes. Do you have a ____*peeler*____?

2. We need to grate the cheese. Do you have the _____?

3. I'll mix the eggs and sugar. Do you have the _____?

4. I like steamed vegetables, so I bought a new _____.

5. Can you slice the bread? Here's the _____.

6. You need to beat the eggs for a long time. Use the _____.

A **Complete the story. Use the words in the box.**

secret ingredient	stirred everything	away the groceries
~~was the best cook~~	family secret	and peeled it

My Favorite Dish

When I was a child in Russia, my aunt Tanya _____was the best cook_____
in the family. Every Saturday, we went to the supermarket. She always
bought the freshest fruit. At home, she got things ready while I put

_____.
          2

Aunt Tanya's fruit cake was my favorite dish. First, she washed the fruit

_____. Then she put all the other ingredients in a bowl,
          3

and I _____ together. Finally, she put the cake in the oven
          4

and baked it. Her _____ was brown sugar. Sorry, I can't tell
          5

you how much she used. It's a _____.
          6

B **Number the sentences in the correct order.**

Rosa's Recipe for Banana Bread

_____ Put the pan in the oven and cook for 45 minutes.

__1__ Take 4 bananas and peel them.

_____ Stir everything together and pour into a pan.

_____ Cut up the bananas.

_____ Put the bananas in a bowl with 2 eggs, 2 cups of flour, and 1 cup of sugar.

_____ Take the bread out of the oven. Let cool and eat!

C **Rewrite the recipe. Use the sentences in B.**

Rosa's Recipe for Banana Bread	
Take 4 bananas and peel them.	

A Circle the correct words.

Pizza Recipe
1. Take a bowl. Put ((in) / on) flour and the other ingredients.
2. Don't leave (out / off) the salt. Stir it.
3. Chop (up / off) some vegetables.
4. Put them (on / in) the pizza.
5. Turn (in / on) the oven. Bake the pizza for 25 minutes.
6. Take (up / out) the pizza and eat it.

B Read the sentences. Separate the phrasal verbs. Then write the sentences another way. Use the pronouns *it* or *them* for the underlined words.

1. I'll chop up the carrots.
    _I'll chop them up._____

2. Can you figure out these recipes?
    _____

3. Did you pick up the milk on your way home?
    _____

4. I didn't write down the ingredients.
    _____

5. I think we can turn off the stove now.
    _____

6. Did you turn on the oven?
    _____

7. I won't leave out the sugar next time.
    _____

8. Did you put the eggs in the bowl?
    _____

C **Match the questions with the answers.**

_c_ 1. Did you start the car?

_____ 2. Did you find the answer?

_____ 3. Did you forget to add the milk?

_____ 4. Did you buy the newspapers?

_____ 5. Did you copy the phone numbers?

_____ 6. Did you add the apples?

a. Yes, I wrote them down.

b. Yes, I picked them up.

c. Yes, I turned it on.

d. Yes, I put them in.

e. Yes, I left it out.

f. Yes, I figured it out.

D **Complete the sentences. Use the words in the box.**

| for | over | on | ~~off~~ | after |

1. This is our stop. We have to get _____off_____ the bus now.

2. Pam is away on vacation, so I'm looking _____ her cat.

3. I can't find my keys. I have to look _____ them.

4. Do you want to come _____ for dinner next weekend?

5. I'm tired of walking. Let's get _____ the bus.

E **Grammar Boost** **Complete the sentences. Use the correct pronouns for the underlined words.**

1. Did <u>Amalia</u> write down <u>the address</u>?

Yes, _____she wrote it down_____.

2. Did <u>Fred</u> look for <u>the phone numbers</u>?

Yes, _____.

3. Did <u>Mario and you</u> turn off <u>the computer</u>?

Yes, _____.

4. Did <u>Bernard</u> figure out <u>the answers</u>?

Yes, _____.

5. Did <u>Marissa</u> get over <u>her cold</u>?

Yes, _____.

6. Did <u>George and Franco</u> pick up <u>the cake</u>?

Yes, _____.

A Complete the conversation. Use the words in the box.

cut down on	have a question	~~Excuse me~~
try them	are the best	chef doesn't use

Elena: _____Excuse me_____. I _____ about something
           1   2

on the menu. What are your special French fries?

Waiter: We use two different kinds of potatoes.

Elena: Are they very salty?

Waiter: No, the _____ much salt.
                        3

Elena: Good. I'm trying to _____ salt. I'll
                                            4

_____.
         5

Waiter: Excellent choice. Ours _____ in town.
                                              6

B Circle the correct possessive adjectives or possessive pronouns.

1. Mai and Anna are looking for (theirs / (their)) recipes.

2. I have (your / yours). Do you have (my / mine)?

3. (Her / Hers) sandwich was delicious. (Our / Ours) were too spicy.

4. How was (your / yours) soup?

5. Gabriela didn't finish (her / hers) soup. Did Luz finish (her / hers)?

6. (My / Mine) name is Katrina. What's (your / yours)?

C Real-life math Use the bill to answer the questions.

1. How much money should the customers leave
   for a 15% tip? _____
   (Hint: Tip only on the cost of the food and drinks.)

2. If they leave a 15% tip, how much will
   they pay for the food, tax, and tip?

   _____

Check		
2 slices of pizza @ 3.75 each =		$7.50
1 soup @ 2.50 each =		$2.50
1 tea @ 1.50 each =		$1.50
1 lemonade @ 1.15 each =		$1.15
	SUB TOTAL:	$12.65
	Tax:	$1.02
	TOTAL:	$13.67

A Read the article.

Unsafe Food Problems in Greenville Last Year

Population of Greenville 29,800

Dr. Peter Jeffords, head of Greenville Hospital, said today that he is worried about the large number of people in the town of Greenville who got sick last year from unsafe food. "It's a problem everywhere," said Dr. Jeffords. "In fact, much of the U.S. population gets sick from unsafe food every year." Most of these problems are not serious, but some people can get very sick and need to go to the hospital. A very small percentage of people die from bacteria and food poisoning every year. Children under five years old and adults over 65 are more likely than other people to get sick.

We asked Dr. Jeffords what we can do to stay safe. He told us. You can have fun in the kitchen and enjoy your food if you follow these rules:
• Wash your hands.
• Work on a clean counter, and always use clean dishes.

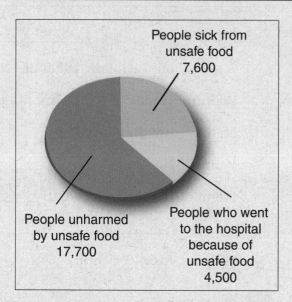

People sick from
unsafe food
7,600

People unharmed
by unsafe food
17,700

People who went
to the hospital
because of
unsafe food
4,500

• Don't work with food when you are sick.
• Don't touch uncooked food with your hands.
• Keep food at safe temperatures. Keep cold food below 41°F. Keep hot food over 140°F.
• Check the "use by" dates. Throw out food that looks or smells bad.

B Mark the sentences T (true) or F (false).

___T___ 1. Every year much of the U.S. population gets sick from food-related diseases.

_____ 2. Young children and older adults are more likely to get sick than the rest of the population.

_____ 3. It is always safe to keep food below 41°F.

_____ 4. Some people who get sick from unsafe food have to go to the hospital.

_____ 5. It's OK to work with food when you're sick.

_____ 6. When food looks or smells bad, it's OK to cook it.

A **Read the essay.**

The Best Chicken Soup in Town

    I love to make chicken soup. Once a month, I make a shopping list and write down the ingredients I need. I always look for the freshest vegetables. I like to put them in the soup.

    When I get home from the supermarket, I check my ingredients carefully. I don't want to leave anything out. I put the chicken in a big pot of hot water and let it cook. Then I chop up onions, carrots, and celery. I put them in the pot and stir in my secret ingredient. Finally, I add noodles or rice.

    When I make my chicken soup, I usually invite my friends to come over to my house for dinner. They say that mine is the best chicken soup in town!

B **Complete the tasks.**

1. Find 3 sentences in the essay with separable phrasal verbs.
   Then write them here.

   _____

   _____

   _____

2. Find 1 sentence in the article with two separable phrasal verbs.
   Then write it here.

   _____

3. Find 2 sentences in the article with inseparable phrasal verbs.
   Then write them here.

   _____

   _____

4. Find a possessive adjective in the article. Then write it here.

   _____

5. Find a possessive pronoun in the article. Then write it here.

   _____

UNIT 7

Money Wise

A Look at the pictures. Match the words with the pictures.

____ security guard   ____ teller   _1_ teller window   ____ loan officer

____ account services desk   ____ open an account   ____ apply for a loan   ____ accounts manager

B Complete the conversation. Use the words in the box.

~~joint account~~   savings account   online banking   direct deposit

1. **Customer:** My wife and I want to share a checking account.

   Accounts Manager: Then you need a _____*joint account*_____.

2. **Customer:** I want to use banking services from my home computer.

   Accounts Manager: That's easy! You can use _____.

3. **Customer:** I want to save money to buy a house.

   Accounts Manager: You should open a _____.

4. **Customer:** I want my paycheck to go directly into my account.

   Accounts Manager: You need _____.

Real-life writing

A **Complete the essay. Use the words in the box.**

save money in	~~is hoping to buy~~	cheaper to bring
reach his goal	financial planning	plans his shopping
doesn't buy lunch	share the cost	

My Brother's Financial Planning

by Luisa Ruiz

My brother Miguel _____is hoping to buy_____
1
a new computer in six months. His old one works, but
it is very slow. Miguel needs a faster computer, so he
can take some online classes. Miguel has a plan. He
has already started to _____ his
2
account at the bank. I also gave him some ideas to help
with his _____.
3

Miguel has learned a lot about saving money. He rides to work with me now, so we
_____ of gas. He _____ at work anymore. Now
4   5
he makes his own lunch because it's _____ it from home. Miguel
6
also _____ carefully. He makes a list of the things he wants. He also
7
uses coupons to save money. Saving money isn't easy, but his financial plan is working.
Soon Miguel will _____ and get a new computer.
8

B **Mark the sentences T (true), F (false), or NI (no information).**

__T__ 1. Luisa's brother wants a new computer.

____ 2. Miguel doesn't have a financial plan.

____ 3. Luisa has a new computer.

____ 4. Miguel doesn't have a bank account.

____ 5. Luisa and Miguel ride to work together.

____ 6. Miguel buys lunch at work.

____ 7. Luisa also makes shopping lists.

____ 8. Miguel's financial plan is working.

A Match the *if* clauses with the main clauses.

<u>d</u> 1. If I have enough money,

____ 2. Ernesto will open a bank account

____ 3. We will go shopping

____ 4. If Anne saves $40 every month,

____ 5. If the sale begins today,

____ 6. They won't buy the car

a. if we need some food.

b. she will have $480 in a year.

c. if it doesn't work well.

d. I will buy a new coat.

e. if he wants to save money.

f. we won't pay the full price.

B Complete the conversation with the future conditional. Use the verbs in parentheses.

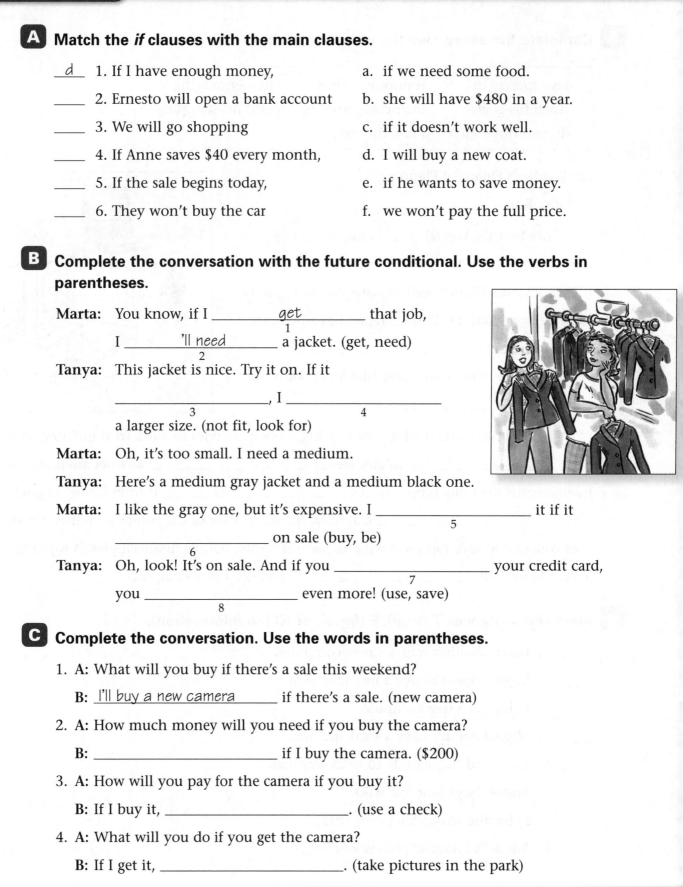

Marta: You know, if I _____<u>get</u>____ that job,

            1

I ____<u>'ll need</u>____ a jacket. (get, need)

        2

Tanya: This jacket is nice. Try it on. If it

_____, I _____

     3   4

a larger size. (not fit, look for)

Marta: Oh, it's too small. I need a medium.

Tanya: Here's a medium gray jacket and a medium black one.

Marta: I like the gray one, but it's expensive. I _____ it if it

                                                  5

_____ on sale (buy, be)

     6

Tanya: Oh, look! It's on sale. And if you _____ your credit card,

                                                      7

you _____ even more! (use, save)

     8

C Complete the conversation. Use the words in parentheses.

1. A: What will you buy if there's a sale this weekend?

  B: <u>I'll buy a new camera</u> if there's a sale. (new camera)

2. A: How much money will you need if you buy the camera?

  B: _____ if I buy the camera. ($200)

3. A: How will you pay for the camera if you buy it?

  B: If I buy it, _____. (use a check)

4. A: What will you do if you get the camera?

  B: If I get it, _____. (take pictures in the park)

D Complete the questions.

1. A: What will Chris do __if he gets a better job__?

   B: If Chris gets a better job, he'll save more money.

2. A: What will he do _____?

   B: If he saves money, he'll buy a computer.

3. A: What will Sara do _____?

   B: If Sara has trouble with her car, she'll look for a new one.

4. A: What will we do _____?

   B: If we find a good car, we'll ask about a car loan.

5. A: What will you do _____?

   B: If I buy a new house, I'll sell the old one.

E 🚀 Grammar Boost Write sentences with the future conditional and *and*. Use the information in the chart.

If...	Mike	Luc
it rains tomorrow	go shopping	stay home
they take a long vacation	travel to South America	drive across the U.S.
they win $1,000	buy a new bicycle	open a savings account
the car doesn't work	ride his bicycle	fix the car
they stay home this weekend	clean the house	make dinner for his friends
there's a sale	not buy anything	buy a cell phone

1. __If it rains tomorrow, Mike will stay home, and Luc will go shopping.__

2. _____

3. _____

4. _____

5. _____

6. _____

A **Complete the conversation. Use the words in the box.**

before we send	talk to my supervisor	~~to report a problem~~
can I help you	that's impossible	When you receive

Sonia: I'm calling ___to report a problem___ on
1
my credit-card bill.

Customer Service: How _____?
2

Sonia: It says I spent $300 at Computer Town

Electronics, but _____.
3
I didn't buy anything there.

Customer Service: OK. I'll _____ and ask
4
her to review it _____
5
your next statement.

Sonia: So I don't have to pay the charges this month?

Customer Service: No. Let's wait and see. _____
6
your next statement, you'll see your new balance.

B **Circle the correct words.**

1. I will check the bank statement (before / (when)) it comes in the mail.

2. We will pay the bill (after / before) we check it.

3. (Before / After) we sign the check, we can get the money.

4. (If / Before) I make a mistake, I'll correct it.

5. In the restaurant, we pay (when / after) we eat.

6. I can save money at the store (if / before) I use coupons.

C **Real-life math** **Answer the questions.**

1. Greg has $3,000 in a savings account. He receives 4% interest on this account.
   How much interest will he earn this year?
   $3,000 × .04 = _____

2. Ana receives 5% interest on her savings account. How much interest will she
   earn this year on $2,500?
   $2,500 × .05 = _____

A Read the article.

Identity Theft at Bank Central

Lakewood—For six months, Noreen Smith, a teller at Bank Central, used her computer to steal bank customers' personal information. Smith then used the information to make credit card purchases. When the bank manager stopped her, she was carrying papers with the names, Social Security numbers, and credit card numbers of several Bank Central customers.

Lakewood mayor Paul Nelson said, "Identity theft is a growing problem in Lakewood and across the U.S. Everyone needs to be careful. This is happening more often."

Mayor Nelson says we should all do the following things to protect ourselves:

1. Shred, or cut up, papers with your bank account numbers and bills with your personal information.

2. Don't carry your Social Security card with you. Don't give people your Social Security number if it isn't really needed.

3. Don't give your personal information on the phone or over the Internet if you don't know the person.

4. Keep your Social Security card and credit cards in a safe place at home.

Mayor Nelson said, "The bank is telling all its customers to check their accounts carefully. We want to make sure everyone's information is safe."

B Circle *a* or *b*.

1. Noreen Smith used her computer to get bank customers' _____.
   a. credit cards
   b. personal information

2. Smith had _____ with her when the bank manager stopped her.
   a. papers with names and numbers
   b. credit card purchases

3. In the article, _____ is talking about identify theft.
   a. the bank manager
   b. the mayor

4. Identify theft is a problem that is getting _____.
   a. smaller
   b. bigger

5. People should keep their Social Security cards and credit cards _____.
   a. with them
   b. in a safe place

6. The article _____ people ways to keep their personal information safe.
   a. tells
   b. doesn't tell

Look at the pictures. Write sentences with the future conditional.

1. If Enrique _____, then he _____ .

(save money)   (buy a car)

If Enrique saves money, he'll buy a car.

2. If he _____, then he _____ .

(buy a car)   (drive to California)

3. If he _____, then he _____ .

(drive to California)   (need more money)

4. If he _____, then he _____ .

(need more money)   (need another job)

5. If he _____, then he _____ .

(need another job)   (look in the want ads)

6. If he _____, then he _____ .

(look in the want ads)   (get a better job)

Living Well

A Look at the picture. Match the pictures with the words.

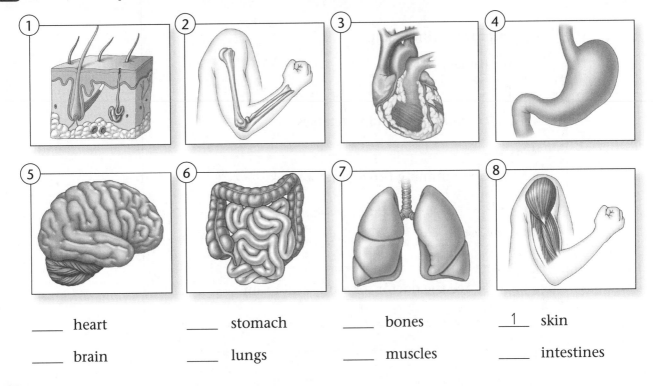

_____ heart   _____ stomach   _____ bones   _1_ skin

_____ brain   _____ lungs   _____ muscles   _____ intestines

B Match the statements with the hospital department names.

_b_ 1. Could you check on Mr. Allison in room 224?
It's time for his medicine.

_____ 2. Congratulations! You have a baby girl!

_____ 3. Mrs. Patel, your son has a bad cold. I'll give him some
medicine.

_____ 4. We're going to do some tests to check your heart.

_____ 5. The ambulance is arriving from the car accident!

_____ 6. We'll take some x-rays of your arm and see if it is broken.

a. cardiology

b. nurse's station

c. emergency

d. pediatrics

e. maternity

f. radiology

A **Complete the outline. Use the sentences in the box. Use capital letters.**

Get in Shape	Manage stress.	See the dentist for cleanings.
Lift weights.	~~Eat low-fat food.~~	Make medical and dental appointments.

Wellness Plan

I. Improve Eating Habits

    A. Eat less fast food.

    B. _____ Eat low-fat food. _____
                    1

    C. Eat more fruit and vegetables.

II. _____
              2

    A. Go swimming three times a week.

    B. _____
               3

III. Stay Well

    A. _____
               4

       1. See the doctor for a physical exam.

       2. _____
               5

    B. _____
               6

B **Look at the outline in A. Where do these points belong? Write *I*, *II*, or *III*.**

_I_ 1. Eat apples, carrots, and lettuce.

____ 2. Don't worry too much about little things.

____ 3. Play some sports.

____ 4. Follow your doctor's advice.

____ 5. Take a long walk.

____ 6. Don't eat too many hamburgers or French fries.

____ 7. Relax sometimes.

____ 8. Exercise several times a week.

A **Read the paragraph. Underline the examples of** *used to*.

My cousin Julia is in great shape now, but she wasn't in the past. She <u>used to</u> be very sick and tired all the time. She <u>didn't use to</u> eat three meals a day. Sometimes she only ate once a day! She <u>used to</u> eat out often, but now she makes her own meals at home. She really enjoys cooking now. Julia didn't like sports, so she <u>didn't use to</u> exercise much. Now, she runs or jogs every morning. She's not tired anymore. She <u>used to</u> look sad and worried, but now she's happy. She <u>used to</u> think that exercise was boring, but she doesn't now. She's healthy and happy. She feels great.

B **Read the sentences about what Julia does now but didn't do in the past. Write sentences with the correct forms of** *used to*.

1. Julia exercises a lot.

   <u>Julia didn't use to exercise a lot.</u>

2. She doesn't watch TV all the time.

   _____

3. She eats salads.

   _____

4. She doesn't eat a lot of junk food.

   _____

5. She doesn't stay inside all day.

   _____

6. She works outside.

   _____

C **Complete the answers.**

1. **A:** Did Bob use to work in Boston?

   B: Yes, <u>he used to work in Boston</u> .

2. **A:** Did he use to take the subway to school?

   B: No, _____ .

3. **A:** Did your friends use to live near here?

   B: Yes, _____ .

4. **A:** Did they use to play sports?

   B: No, _____ .

5. **A:** Did you use to take a walk every day?

   B: Yes, _____ .

6. **A:** Did you use to get enough sleep?

   B: No, _____ .

D Complete the questions. Use the correct form of *used to* and the words in parentheses.

1. Where ___did Rafael use to play tennis___? (Rafael/play tennis)

2. How often _____? (he/practice)

3. Where _____? (Liz/exercise)

4. What _____? (you/eat for lunch)

5. How often _____? (you/go to the gym)

6. Why _____? (Katya/eat fast food)

7. Where _____? (Joe/study)

8. How _____? (Lara/save money)

E **Grammar Boost** Complete the sentences. Use the simple past or *used to.*

1. I ___watched___ TV yesterday. (watch)

   I ___used to watch___ TV every night when I was younger.

2. I _____ my bike to school last week. (ride)

   I _____ my bike to school every day when I was younger.

3. I _____ only one cup of coffee this morning. (drink)

   I _____ four cups of coffee every day.

4. I _____ soccer with my friends last Saturday. (not play)

   I _____ soccer in high school.

5. I _____ to bed early last night. (go)

   I _____ to bed early when I was ten years old.

6. I _____ for the grammar test on Monday. (not study)

   I _____ for tests in high school.

7. I _____ this week. (not exercise)

   I _____ every day in college.

8. I _____ pizza for lunch today. (eat)

   I _____ pizza a lot last year.

A **Complete the conversation. Use the words in the box.**

under a lot of	Why don't you	~~a little concerned about~~
give it a try	I used to go	Have you been getting

Dr. Stetson: I'm <u>a little concerned about</u> your blood pressure.

1

Mrs. Choi: I've been _____ stress recently.

2

Dr. Stetson: _____ enough sleep?

3

Mrs. Choi: Well, doctor, _____ to bed early, but now

4

I just can't sleep.

Dr. Stetson: _____ walk after dinner.

5

Mrs. Choi: OK. I'll _____. I'll start tonight.

6

B **Complete the sentences with the present perfect continuous. Use the words in parentheses.**

1. Mrs. Choi _____<u>has been sleeping</u>_____ better since she saw the doctor. (sleep)

2. She _____ as stressed. (not feel)

3. She and her husband _____ every night after dinner. (walk)

4. Her children _____ about how well she looks. (talk)

5. Her husband _____ happier, too. (act)

C **Real-life math** **Read about Sara. Write the answers to the questions. Use the chart.**

Sara had a busy weekend. On Saturday morning, she took care of her friend's children for two hours. In the afternoon, she went on a 90-minute bike ride.

On Sunday Sara went to the gym. She went swimming for one hour and lifted weights for 30 minutes.

Activity	Calories/hour
swimming	320
bike riding	350
taking care of children	200
lifting weights	180

1. How many calories did Sara burn on Saturday? _____

2. How many calories did she burn on Sunday? _____

3. Did Sara burn more calories on Saturday or Sunday? _____

4. Which activity burned the most calories? _____

A Read the prescription label.

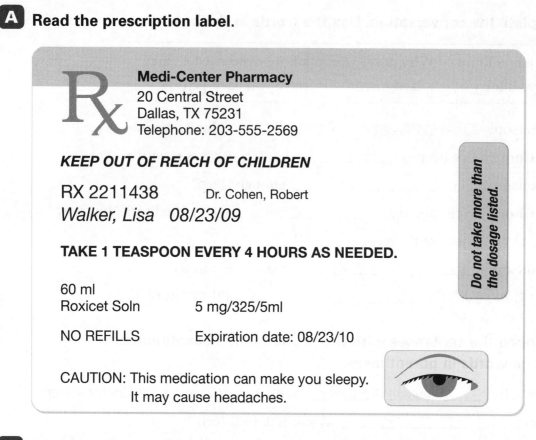

> **R**x **Medi-Center Pharmacy**
> 20 Central Street
> Dallas, TX 75231
> Telephone: 203-555-2569
>
> **KEEP OUT OF REACH OF CHILDREN**
>
> RX 2211438   Dr. Cohen, Robert
> *Walker, Lisa   08/23/09*
>
> **TAKE 1 TEASPOON EVERY 4 HOURS AS NEEDED.**
>
> 60 ml
> Roxicet Soln   5 mg/325/5ml
>
> NO REFILLS   Expiration date: 08/23/10
>
> CAUTION: This medication can make you sleepy.
>   It may cause headaches.
>
> *Do not take more than the dosage listed.*

B Mark the sentences T (true), F (false), or NI (no information).

<u>F</u> 1. The prescription number is 203555-2569

_____ 2. The medicine is for Lisa Walker.

_____ 3. She can take one teaspoon every four hours.

_____ 4. She needs to eat something before she takes the medicine.

_____ 5. She can get one refill of this medicine.

_____ 6. The medicine may make her sleepy.

_____ 7. This is a generic medicine.

_____ 8. The medicine is safe for children.

A **Write answers to the questions. Use the correct form of *used to* and your own information.**

When you were 8 years old, what did you do?

1. What school did you use to go to?

   <u>I used to go to Belleville Primary School.</u>

2. What programs did you use to watch on TV?

   _____

3. What games did you and your friends use to play together?

   _____

4. How did you use to get to school?

   _____

5. What time did you use to get up in the morning?

   _____

6. What time did you use to go to bed at night?

   _____

7. Where did you use to go on vacation?

   _____

8. What did you use to do on vacations?

   _____

9. What sports did you use to play?

   _____

10. Who used to be your favorite singer?

   _____

B **Look at your answers in A. Choose one answer and write a paragraph on your own paper about what you used to do.**

   <u>   When I was eight years old, I used to go on vacations with</u>
   <u>my family. We used to travel to my grandmother's house in Miami....</u>

Hit the Road

LESSON 1 Vocabulary

A Match the words with the pictures.

____ headlight ____ license plate ____ windshield ____ tire __1__ hood

____ trunk ____ gas tank ____ steering wheel ____ horn ____ bumper

B Match the sentences with the parts of the car.

__c__ 1. Your owner's manual is in here.   a. speedometer

____ 2. Use this to see if anyone is behind you.   b. steering wheel

____ 3. This will show you how fast you are going.   c. glove compartment

____ 4. Keep both hands on it when you're driving.   d. horn

____ 5. Use this to warn other drivers if they don't see you.   e. ignition

____ 6. Put the key in this to start the car.   f. rearview mirror

A **Complete the story. Use the words in the box.**

be sure to take	take my advice	~~like to travel~~
stayed there for two	be ready to	we took a train trip
you can see	and comfortable	favorite part of

Niagara Falls – An Amazing Trip

My brother and I _____ like to travel _____ by train. When
                                    1

you travel by train, _____ everything around
                                    2

you. It's fast _____ , and you don't have to
                            3

watch the roads, maps, or the other cars.

   Last summer, _____ to Niagara Falls, New

York. We _____
                    5

days. First, we went to the state park and walked on the

trails. We stopped to see the falls and take some pictures.

The falls are incredible!

   The next day, we took a boat, the Maid of the Mist,

to the falls. You should do it sometime. It was definitely

my _____ the trip.
                    6

We really enjoyed the boat ride but _____ .
                                                    7

If you go on the Maid of the Mist, _____ get
                                                    8

wet! Also, _____ a camera. You'll want to take
                        9

a lot of pictures.

B **Write answers to the questions.**

1. The writer went to Niagara
   Falls by ____.

   a. car

   b. train *(circled)*

2. The writer traveled with ____.

   a. his cousin

   b. his brother

3. They walked on the ____.

   a. falls

   b. trails

4. The writer's favorite part of the trip
   was ____.

   a. the boat ride

   b. the train trip

A Match the clauses to make sentences.

_c_ 1. When Ana looks at the engine,   a. he fixed the mirrors.

____ 2. Before he started the car,   b. they'll go to the gym.

____ 3. He found the problem   c. she always checks the oil.

____ 4. I asked about the starter   d. when he stopped the car.

____ 5. Before we fix a problem,   e. when I took the car to the mechanic.

____ 6. After they wash the car,   f. we read about it in the owner's manual.

B Put the events in each sentence in order. Write *first* or *second*. If the events happen at the same time, write *same*.

1. I called Sak before I went to class.

   _____first_____   _____second_____

2. Before Dennis takes a long car trip, he checks everything on his car.

   _____   _____

3. Pat picked up her car after the mechanic called.

   _____   _____

4. I turn on the headlights when it is dark.

   _____   _____

5. We look at the tires before we get in the car,

   _____   _____

6. Trong looked at the map after we got lost.

   _____   _____

C Circle the correct words.

1. Nati will check the map ((before)/ after) she takes a trip.

2. She will have a mechanic look at the car (after / before) she leaves.

3. (When / Before) she is on the road, she'll stop every two hours for a break.

4. She always brings a map (after / when) she takes a trip.

5. Fatah and Rachid didn't check the gas tank (after / before) they went on their trip.

D Write answers to the questions. Use the words in parentheses and complete sentences.

1. When did you study? (before, come to class)

   <u>I studied before I came to class.</u>

2. When does Sao change the oil in his car? (before, take a trip)

   _____

3. When will Irina call? (after, pick up her car)

   _____

4. When do you hear the noise? (when, turn left)

   _____

5. When does Otto use the turn signal? (before, make a turn)

   _____

E 🚀 **Grammar Boost** **Complete the paragraphs with the simple present, simple past, or future. Use the verbs in parentheses.**

Brian started a car trip this morning, but things are not going well. When he got to his car, he _____<u>saw</u>_____
that his front tire _____ flat. (see, be)
                                    2
Also, he didn't check the map before he

_____ home. (leave) Now he's
            3
lost and his car has stopped. It doesn't start when he

_____ the ignition. (turn on)
            4
His gas tank is empty!

Brian got out of the car to check the map and make a phone call. He didn't close the door of the car when he _____. (get out) Oh no! Brian will have more
                                                          5
problems when that big car _____ the door! (hit)
                                        6

A **Complete the conversation. Use the words in the box.**

to my manager	How much	don't work	two-year warranty
work something out	It's going for	doesn't either	~~It has only~~

Car dealer: This is a fantastic car. _____It has only_____ 25,000 miles on it,
1

and it has a _____.
2

Daniel: It sure is nice. _____ is it?
3

Car dealer: _____ $9,500. It's a terrific price.
4

Daniel: $9,500! But the headlights _____, and the radio
5

_____!
6

Car dealer: Uhhh... Let me talk _____. I'm sure we can
7

_____.
8

B **Complete the sentences with *and, too, either,* or *but*.**

1. The headlights work, _____but_____ the turn signals don't.

2. The radio doesn't work, _____ the lights don't either.

3. I like the car, and my brother likes it, _____.

4. The car has a CD player, _____ it doesn't have a radio.

5. The tires don't look good, and the windshield doesn't _____.

C **Real-life math** **Read the problems. Answer the questions.**

1. Amarjit drives 15,000 miles per year. His car gets 30 miles per gallon. The average price of gas last year was $3.10 per gallon. How much did Amarjit spend on gas last year? _____

2. Lilia also drives 15,000 miles per year. Her car gets 34 miles per gallon. The average price of gas last year was the same $3.10 per gallon. How much did Lilia spend on gas last year?

_____

3. Who spent more money on gas: Amarjit or Lilia?

_____

Need help?

Total cost = Total miles ÷ miles per gallon x price

A   Read the letters.

Ask Chris, The Car Guy

Dear Chris,
    I need to buy a used car, but I want to be sure I don't get a lemon. What should I do?
                Needs Wheels

Dear Needs Wheels,
    If you buy a used car from a dealer, the lemon laws will cover you in most states. But check the laws in your state because not all states have exactly the same laws. And have a mechanic check out any used car for problems before you buy. Good luck!
                   Chris

Dear Chris,
    I bought a new car last year. But now, after 15,000 miles, it isn't working very well. I've taken it to the mechanic for the ignition, the headlights, and the tires. Every few weeks, it's something different. Do I have a lemon?
          Worn Out and Tired

Dear Worn Out and Tired,
    Maybe yes, maybe no. Has the mechanic fixed each of the different problems? If so, then you just have a car with a lot of different problems. Have you taken the car in for the same problem three or four times? If so, then you might have a lemon. Keep a record of each problem, the date, the repair cost, the mechanic or garage, and the work done. A repair log can show you if your car is a lemon or not.
                   Chris

Dear Chris,
    What should I look for when I take a car for a test drive?
          Millie Shoemaker

Dear Millie,
    Drive the car on local streets, on the highway, and in traffic. Are you comfortable in the car? Can you see all around? Is the car quiet or noisy? Check the warranty on the car, too. If it's a used car, check the repair and maintenance log. Every dealer and car is different. I hope you find a car that fits your needs.
                   Chris

B   Mark the sentences T (true), F (false), or NI (no information).

  _F_   1. Lemon laws protect all cars.

  ____   2. Always ask a mechanic to check a used car.

  ____   3. All states have the same laws about lemons.

  ____   4. If a car has a lot of problems, it is a lemon.

  ____   5. Chris is a mechanic.

  ____   6. A repair and maintenance log records car problems and work done.

A Read the travel journal.

July 12
We are packed and ready to drive to Nashville, TN. Before we started packing, we took the car to the mechanic. We always take the car to our mechanic before we take a long car trip.

July 13

After we finished breakfast, we left Chicago. We drove south on Route 65 through Indiana. We stopped for lunch in Louisville, Kentucky. After lunch, we continued for about another four hours. Finally, we arrived in Nashville. When we got there, we found our motel and ate dinner. We went to bed early. We were really tired.

July 14
Nashville is not a large city, but there's a lot to do there. There are a lot of music stores and music museums. We took a bus tour of the city, and we went to the Country Music Hall of Fame, too. We also saw the Grand Ole Opry[1] and walked around the stores. It was late so we didn't have time to go into many stores, and we didn't have time to buy any souvenirs, either. After dinner, we went to a club to listen to some country music. Tomorrow, we'll visit Centennial Park before we go home.

[1] Grand Ole Opry: a famous country music concert hall

B Complete the tasks below.

1. Look at Joanie's journal for July 13. Find two sentences with a time clause in the simple past. Write it here.

   <u>After we finished breakfast, we left Chicago.</u>
   _____

2. Look at Joanie's journal for July 12. Find a sentence with a time clause in the simple present. Write it here.

   _____

3. Find a sentence with *but*. Write it here.

   _____

4. Look at Joanie's journal for July 14. Find a sentence with a time clause in the future. Write it here.

   _____

5. Find a sentence with *and…too*. Write it here.

   _____

6. Find a sentence with *and…either*. Write it here.

   _____

Crime Doesn't Pay

A Look at the pictures. Complete the safety flyer. Use the words in the box.

walk alone	~~Lock the doors~~	commit a crime	Walk in
report it	arrest a suspect	Protect your wallet	

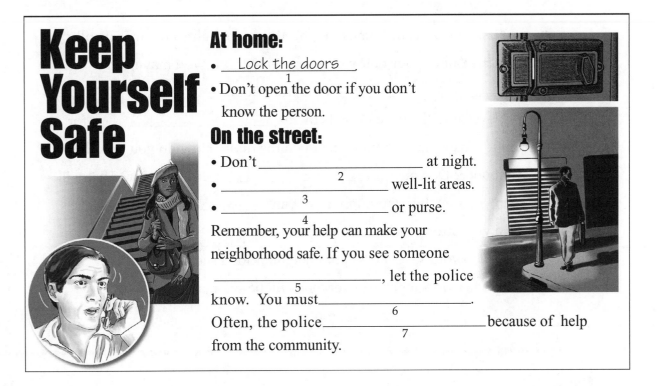

Keep Yourself Safe

At home:
- ___Lock the doors___ .
  1
- Don't open the door if you don't know the person.

On the street:
- Don't _____ at night.
                    2
- _____ well-lit areas.
         3
- _____ or purse.
         4

Remember, your help can make your neighborhood safe. If you see someone _____, let the police
                    5
know. You must_____.
                         6
Often, the police_____because of help
                              7
from the community.

B Match the roles with the definitions.

_e_ 1. The witnesses   a. is the twelve people who decide to the case.

____ 2. The defendant   b. is the person who listens to the case.

____ 3. The attorney   c. is the place where the trial is.

____ 4. The jury   d. is the person on trial.

____ 5. The judge   e. are the people who tell what they saw.

____ 6. The courtroom   f. is the person who questions the witnesses.

A Complete the article. Use the words in the box.

to install a deadbolt lock	a peephole	home security
better lighting	sleep better	have a chain lock

Making Your Home a Safe Place

Have you ever thought about how to make your home a safer place to live? If you have, then you need to learn about ___home security___.
                                    1

First, look at your home at night. When the lights are on, is it still dark in front of your house or apartment? If it is, you may need to have _____ at the front door.
                              2

Next, close the front door. Is there _____, for
                                                    3
you to look through before you open the door? How do you lock the front door? Do you _____ for the door? That will
                                    4
keep you safe, but you might also want _____.
                                                          5
It's a very strong lock.

Talk to your neighbors about neighborhood security. If everyone works together, everyone will be safer, and you'll _____, too.
              6

B Circle the correct words.

1. **A:** You should make your home safer.

   B: I know. I'll ((install better lighting) / sleep better) at my front door.

2. **A:** That's a good idea. What about your front door?

   B: I think I'll get a (peephole / deadbolt lock), so I can see who's there before I open the door.

3. **A:** You might also want to get a (better lighting / deadbolt lock) for the door.

   B: That's a good idea. I think I'll (sleep better / close the door) when I make these safety improvements.

A Read the brochure. Underline 6 sentences with gerunds as subjects.

New Ideas from Code One

Code One's newest security system, Safety First, is making homes, offices, schools, and other buildings safer for everyone.

<u>Keeping you safe is our most important job.</u> Using our new system will make it more difficult for people to break in. People all around the state are protecting their homes and businesses with Safety First.

Entering a dark building at night doesn't have to be a problem. Using our lighting system is easy. With Safety First, people can turn on the lights before they enter. Our new system makes it easy to get help when you need it. Pushing just one button on your phone calls the police for you. Reporting a crime is faster than ever before.

Come and check out how Safety First home security system can help your family, friends, and co-workers safe and happy! Staying safe is easy with Safety First.

B Complete the sentences. Use the underlined verbs in the first sentence to make gerunds.

1. Kara <u>locks</u> the windows every night.

   <u>Locking</u> the windows is the right thing to do.

2. She <u>knows</u> most of her neighbors.

   _____ most of her neighbors is important.

3. She doesn't <u>walk</u> alone at night.

   _____ alone at night can be dangerous.

4. She's going to <u>install</u> stronger locks on the door.

   _____ stronger locks on the door is a good idea.

5. She doesn't <u>carry</u> a lot of money.

   _____ a lot of money is not a good idea.

6. She never <u>lets</u> strangers in her house.

   _____ strangers in your house isn't safe.

C Read the sentences. Write *G* for gerund or *P* for present continuous.

   _P_ 1. The judge is listening to the questions and answers.

   ____ 2. Telling the truth is important in court.

   ____ 3. One witness is explaining what she saw.

   ____ 4. She's answering the attorney's questions.

   ____ 5. Making a decision is not always easy.

   ____ 6. The jury is thinking about what they heard.

D **Complete the sentences. Use a gerund or present continuous form.**

1. The people _____*are watching*_____ their neighborhood. (watch)

2. _____ lights is a good idea. (turn on)

3. Everyone _____ sure their neighbors are safe. (make)

4. Right now, I _____ a new lock. (install)

5. _____ crimes can save lives. (report)

6. _____ our neighborhood is everyone's job. (protect)

E 🚀 **Grammar Boost** **Look at the picture. What is Susan doing wrong? Complete the sentences with the present continuous or gerunds as subjects. Use the words in parentheses.**

1. (not turn on the lights)

   Susan _*isn't turning on the lights.*_

   _*Not turning on*_____ the lights is a mistake.

2. (not lock the doors)

   Susan _____ .

   _____ can be dangerous.

3. (not watch other people)

   Susan _____ .

   _____ is a bad idea.

4. (not put down her coffee)

   Susan _____ .

   _____ is a mistake.

> **Grammar note**
>
> ***Negative Gerunds***
> To form a negative gerund
> as subject, use *not* + gerund.

A **Complete the conversation. Use the words in the box.**

like to report	First, they broke	after that	what happened
suddenly they ran	a complete report	Reporting this	~~How can I direct~~

Officer: Police Department. _____How can I direct_____ your call?
₁

Witness: I'd _____ a crime I witnessed.
₂

Officer: Can you tell me _____?
₃

Witness: Well, I was parking my car when I saw two men across the street.

_____ the window of Grant's Electronics.
₄

Then they took a TV.

Officer: What happened _____?
₅

Witness: I think they saw me because they dropped the TV and

_____ away.
₆

Officer: OK. Hold on, please. Another officer will fill out _____.
₇

_____ was the right thing to do.
₈

B **Circle the correct words.**

1. It's not safe to ((leave) / leaving) the windows open when you go out.

2. (Driving / Drive) alone at night can be dangerous.

3. It's a good idea to (lock / locking) the door when you get in the car.

4. It's good to (carry / carrying) a cell phone with you.

C **Real-life math** **Study the survey. Answer the questions.**

A survey asked 1,000 people what crimes they were most worried about.

1. What crime are people most worried about?

_____

2. What crime are people least worried about?

_____

3. How many people are worried about
someone breaking into their home?

_____

What Are You Worried About?

- someone breaking into your home: 31%
- someone stealing your car: 14%
- someone hurting you: 18%
- someone hurting your child: 37%

A Read the job ads.

Help Wanted

Animal Control Worker	Fire Inspector	Driver's License Examiner
Salary: $23,305, full-time position Duties[1] include: picking up animals that are lost, sick, or dangerous; investigating reports of animal abuse. Qualifications[2]: high school diploma or GED; driver's license. Must enjoy working with animals. Benefits: available for full-time employees. To apply: call 555-3211.	Salary: $25 per hour, full-time position Duties include: checking buildings for problems that can cause fires, investigating the causes of fires. Qualifications: 5 years experience as a firefighter. College degree preferred. Must be able to solve problems. Benefits: available for full-time employees. To apply: call 555-6789.	Salary: $10.00 per hour, part-time position. Duties include: testing people's driving skills. Qualifications: state driver's license and high school diploma. To apply call: 555-0404

[1] duties: what you do at work
[2] qualifications: the skills needed for a job

B Read about the people. Answer the questions.

1. Barbara has her driver's license. She's 21 years old, and she likes to work with animals. Which job should she apply for?

   _____

2. Reda has a college degree. He has worked as a firefighter for 6 years. Which job should he apply for?

   _____

3. Lena cannot work full time. She enjoys working with people. She is a great driver and has her high school diploma. Which job should she apply for?

   _____

A **Look at the pictures. Read the script.**

Welcome to *Real-Life Crime* with Officer Bob. We start off tonight on a quiet evening. A woman is walking home from the bank. She's just cashed her paycheck. It's dark. Walking alone at night can be scary. It can also be dangerous. She hears a noise. Her hands are shaking as she opens her front door.

What can you do to make sure you don't become a crime victim? Following some simple safety rules can protect everyone from crime.

- It's a good idea to walk with a friend.
- It's important to find other people and a lighted area. Most criminals wait in dark places.
- It isn't safe to carry a lot of money with you.

We hope that you will think about what you have seen and heard on this program so you don't become a victim of a crime. Remember, watching the people around you can keep you safe.

B **Look at A. Complete these tasks.**

1. Find three examples of gerunds as subjects. Write them here.

_____

_____

_____

2. Find two examples of the present continuous. Write them here.

_____

_____

3. Find three examples of infinitives. Write them here.

_____

_____

_____

That's Life

Vocabulary

A Match the sentences with the life events.

  _c_   1. That's great! When will the wedding be?

_____ 2. Congratulations! It's a boy!

_____ 3. What are you planning to do now that you're finished with school?

_____ 4. Congratulations! You started as assistant manager, and now you're the manager!

_____ 5. I can't believe it! Now my daughter has a daughter.

_____ 6. After 40 years at work, now you can relax!

a. get a promotion

b. retire

c. get engaged

d. become a grandparent

e. have a baby

f. graduate

B Look at the newspaper announcements. Complete the sentences. Use the words in the box.

Birth   funeral   Death   ~~Wedding~~   married   born

Johnsbury News **Section C**

Wedding
_____ **ANNOUNCEMENTS**
  1

Hannah and Peter Chavez

Hannah and Peter Chavez were _____
  2
on July 20th. Both the bride and the groom graduated from Johnsbury High School last spring. The couple plans to live in Bradford.

_____ **ANNOUNCEMENTS**
  3

RICCIO – Sara Maria Riccio was _____
  4
on July 29 to Blanca and Daniel Riccio.

_____ **NOTICES**
  5

Robert Howland

Robert Howland, age 95, died on August 10th. A _____ service is planned for August
  6
14th at Wellwood Funeral Home.

A Complete the responses. Use the words in the box.

~~Congratulations on your~~	can bring anything	a great party	can't make it
are looking forward	excited to come	out of town	for inviting us

Dear Charley and Ginger,

      Congratulations on your new jobs! I'm sorry, but I _____
                        1   2
to your party. I'm going to be _____. I hope you have
                                          3
_____. I'll see you soon. I want to hear all about your jobs.
          4

Love,
Felipe

Dear Charley and Ginger,

      We're so glad to hear about your new jobs. Congratulations! Thanks

_____ to your party. We are so _____.
              5   6
We _____ to seeing you both. Please let us know if we
            7

_____.
      8

See you then,
Daniel and Jennifer

B Read the invitation. Circle *a* or *b*.

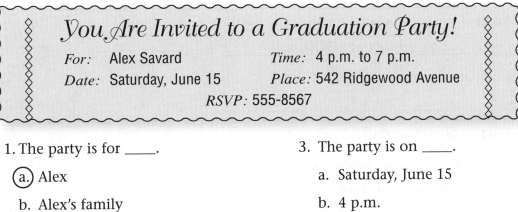

You Are Invited to a Graduation Party!

For: Alex Savard   *Time:* 4 p.m. to 7 p.m.
Date: Saturday, June 15   *Place:* 542 Ridgewood Avenue
RSVP: 555-8567

1. The party is for ____.
   a. Alex
   b. Alex's family

2. The party is a celebration of a ____.
   a. wedding
   b. graduation

3. The party is on ____.
   a. Saturday, June 15
   b. 4 p.m.

4. The party is at ____.
   a. 542 Ridgewood Avenue
   b. Saturday, June 15

A **Complete the sentences. Use the present passive and the verbs in parentheses.**

1. Every year, all our friends and relatives _____are invited_____ to a party to celebrate my parents' anniversary. (invite)

2. Invitations _____ by email. (send)

3. Our house _____ by my brothers and sisters. (decorate)

4. The food _____ by my aunts and uncles. (prepare)

5. The music _____ by my brother's band. (perform)

6. Pictures _____ by a friend. (take)

B **Write answers to the questions. Use the present passive and complete sentences.**

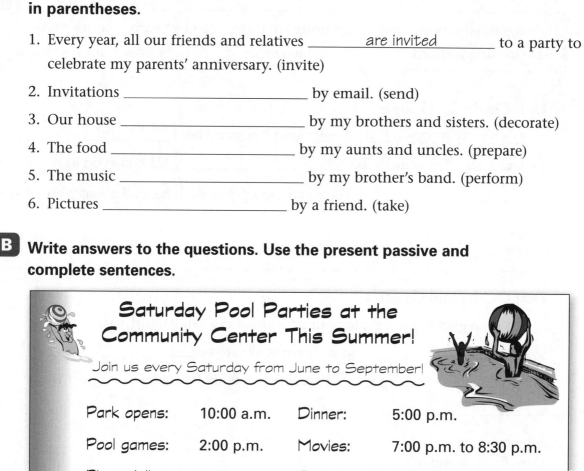

Saturday Pool Parties at the Community Center This Summer!

Join us every Saturday from June to September!

Park opens:	10:00 a.m.	Dinner:	5:00 p.m.
Pool games:	2:00 p.m.	Movies:	7:00 p.m. to 8:30 p.m.
Pizza delivery:	4:45 p.m.	Pool closes:	9:00 p.m.

1. When is the park opened for the pool parties?

_____It's opened at 10:00._____

2. When are the pizzas delivered?

_____

3. When is dinner served?

_____

4. When are the movies shown?

_____

5. When is the pool closed?

_____

C **Rewrite the sentences. Use the present passive with *by*.**

1. Maggie picks the flowers for the weddings.

   The flowers are picked by Maggie.

2. Celia delivers the flowers.

   _____

3. A professional photographer takes the pictures.

   _____

4. The Jones Family Jazz Band performs the music.

   _____

5. Barry's Bake Shop bakes the wedding cakes.

   _____

6. The Green Meadows Restaurant prepares and serves the meals.

   _____

D **Grammar Boost** **Read the list. Then complete the paragraph with the present passive and *already* or *yet*.**

Wedding "To Do" List		
	Done	Not done
1. clean the house		✗
2. make the cake	✓	
3. decorate the backyard	✓	
4. wrap the gifts	✓	
5. wash the glasses		✗
6. prepare the food		✗

Grammar note

Already
Use *already* to talk about some time before now. *Already* comes before the past participle or at the end of the sentence.

Yet
Use *yet* to talk about some time up to now. With negative sentences, *yet* comes at the end of the sentence.

My sister's wedding is today! We've done a lot of things, but there is still so much to do before the wedding. I need to keep a list. The wedding will be at our house, but the house ____isn't cleaned yet____. The cake _____. It looks great,
                    1   2
and I hope it tastes good, too. The backyard _____. We did that last
                                                    3
night. The gifts _____. We have enough plates and glasses, but the
                    4
glasses _____. The food _____. My mother and
              5   6
aunts are in the kitchen cooking right now. I hope we finish everything by 2:00. That's when the wedding begins.

LESSON 4 · Everyday conversation

A Complete the conversation. Use the words in the box.

| That's great | I'll be able to | ~~got some good news~~ |
| too bad | Let's celebrate | the bad |

Todd: Hello, Fong? It's Todd. I've ___*got some good news*___ and some bad news.
₁

Fong: Oh, no. What's _____ news?
₂

Todd: Well, I took my GED today. It was really hard.

Fong: Oh, no. That's _____.
₃

Todd: Yes, but the good news is that I passed. Now _____ apply for
₄
that manager's job at the restaurant.

Fong: Congratulations! _____ news! _____
₅ ₆
tonight.

Todd: OK. I'll be home in a little while.

B Complete the sentences with *be able to* and the verbs in parentheses.

1. **A:** I hope you _____*were able to go*_____ to the bank yesterday. (go)

   B: No, I wasn't. I _____ my paycheck. (not find)

2. **A:** Rick _____ to Maria's wedding next week. (not go)

   B: That's too bad. He _____ my graduation party last
   month either. (not attend)

3. **A:** Good luck on your test tonight. I'm sure you _____
   easily. (pass) You studied very hard.

   B: Well, I _____ all the practice problems last night, so I'm
   a little worried. (not finish)

C Real-life math   Read about Mei and Jack. Answer the questions.

1. Mei and Jack are planning a retirement party for
   their father. Look at their budget and plans. How
   many people will they be able to invite to the party?

   _____

2. If they want to invite 10 more people, how much will the
   party cost? _____

> Retirement Party for Dad
> Budget: $2,000
> Room: $225
> Band: $275
> Dinner: $15 per person,
>   including the tip

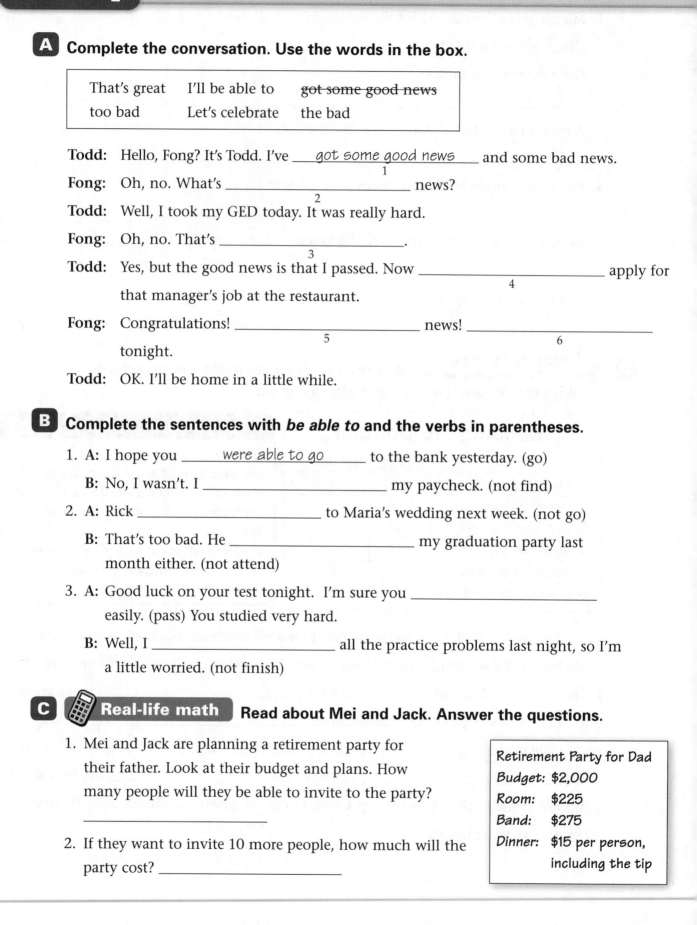

A **Read the brochure.**

To Buy or To Rent?
That Is the Question

So you want to have your own home?
Should you buy or rent?

If you buy,
you can make any changes you want to. You own it. It's yours. All the money you spend on your house goes to you.

But...
You are responsible for doing the repairs on the house. You may need to make a large down payment on your mortgage.[1]

If you rent,
you are not responsible for doing the repairs. Your security deposit[2] will be lower than the down payment[3] on a mortgage.

But...
You may have to ask the landlord if you can make changes. It doesn't belong to you. All the money you spend on rent goes to the landlord.

Here are some things you should think about before you rent or buy:

1. How much money can you pay each month?

2. What do you need and want in a home?

3. What kind of neighborhood do you want to live in?

Remember, your race, religion, family status, or disability should not keep you from buying or renting a home. Everyone is protected by the Fair Housing Act.

[1]mortgage: the money you owe on your house
[2]security deposit: money you pay when you rent a house; you get the money back if you leave
[3]down payment: a first payment for something you buy

B **Mark the sentences T (true) or F (false.) If a sentence is false, rewrite it to make it true.**

_F_ 1. You are responsible for doing the repairs if you rent a home.

<u>You are responsible for doing the repairs if you buy a home</u>.

____ 2. You may need to make a large down payment on your mortgage when you buy a house.

_____

____ 3. If you rent a house, you may have to ask the landlord if you can paint it.

_____

____ 4. If you rent a house, it belongs to you.

_____

____ 5. A security deposit is usually larger than a down payment on a mortgage.

_____

A Read the list.

Dan and Linda's Wedding

	To Do	Who Will Do It
✔	print the invitations	
✔	arrange the flowers	
✔	bake the cake	
	take photos	Tran
✔	make the dress	
✔	set the tables	
	serve the food	the waiters
	make the coffee	Gourmet Catering
✔	decorate reception hall	
	greet the guests	Dan and Linda's family

B Look at the list in A. Write sentences about the things that are checked. Use the present passive.

1. *The invitations are printed.* _____

2. _____

3. _____

4. _____

5. _____

6. _____

C Look at the list in A. Write sentences about the things that are not checked off. Use *will be able to* and the information in the chart.

1. *Tran will be able to take the photos.* _____

2. _____

3. _____

4. _____

Doing the Right Thing

LESSON 1 **Vocabulary**

A **Match the words with the pictures.**

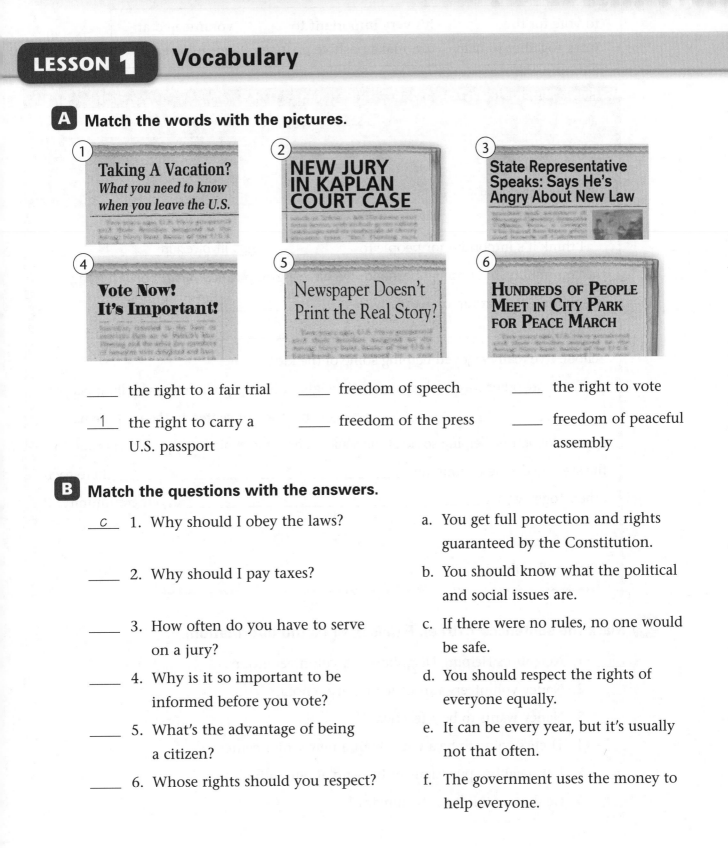

1. Taking A Vacation?
*What you need to know
when you leave the U.S.*

2. **NEW JURY
IN KAPLAN
COURT CASE**

3. State Representative
Speaks: Says He's
Angry About New Law

4. **Vote Now!
It's Important!**

5. Newspaper Doesn't
Print the Real Story?

6. HUNDREDS OF PEOPLE
MEET IN CITY PARK
FOR PEACE MARCH

____ the right to a fair trial ____ freedom of speech ____ the right to vote

_1_ the right to carry a
U.S. passport ____ freedom of the press ____ freedom of peaceful
assembly

B **Match the questions with the answers.**

_c_ 1. Why should I obey the laws?

____ 2. Why should I pay taxes?

____ 3. How often do you have to serve
on a jury?

____ 4. Why is it so important to be
informed before you vote?

____ 5. What's the advantage of being
a citizen?

____ 6. Whose rights should you respect?

a. You get full protection and rights
guaranteed by the Constitution.

b. You should know what the political
and social issues are.

c. If there were no rules, no one would
be safe.

d. You should respect the rights of
everyone equally.

e. It can be every year, but it's usually
not that often.

f. The government uses the money to
help everyone.

A **Complete the letter. Use the words in the box.**

to vote for the	It's very important to	volunteered at
work together to help	can make positive changes	~~get involved in~~

✉ **Email - Message (Plain Text)**   _ □ ×

Reply | Reply to All | Forward | Print | Save | Delete | Previous | Next

From: Nancy Lozada
To: the Editor
Subject: Letter to the Editor

Dear Editor,

I think it's important for people to _____ get involved in _____
1
the community. In our neighborhood, we have a group called Neighbors Helping

Neighbors. It's a group of people who _____
2
each other. I've _____ Deed's Elementary
3
School. I've really enjoyed helping some of the kids.

There are other ways to help, too. My neighbor has a sign in his yard telling people

_____ new senior center. In the past, he has
4
spent a lot of time helping some of the seniors get to the clinic for appointments and to

the store to do their shopping. _____ help each
5
other. Together, we _____ in our community.
6

Nancy Lozada

Libertyville, Illinois

B **Mark the sentences T (true), F (false), or NI (no information).**

__T__ 1. Neighbors Helping Neighbors is a volunteer group.

_____ 2. Nancy volunteers at the elementary school.

_____ 3. Nancy wants to be a teacher.

_____ 4. There's going to be a vote about a new senior center.

_____ 5. Her neighbor puts signs in his yard about voting.

_____ 6. He drives seniors to the movies.

A Read the schedule. Complete the sentences with infinitives.

Danville Community Festival

Time	Activity	Volunteers to work
10:00-2:00	sell tickets	Malik
11:00	start race	Mark
11:00-1:00	run	Jim, Renee
12:00-2:00	serve food	Pavel, Ines
2:00	announce winner	Mark
4:00-5:00	clean up	all

1. Malik volunteered _____ to sell _____ tickets at 10:00.

2. At 11:00, Mark is planning _____ the race.

3. Jim and Renee decided _____ in the race from 11:00 to 1:00.

4. Pavel and Ines agreed _____ food for two hours.

5. At 2:00, Mark needs _____ the winner of the race.

6. From 4:00 to 5:00, all the volunteers are planning _____.

B Answer the questions. Use the words in parentheses.

1. **A:** What does Betsy want to do tomorrow? (go to the mall)

   B: _She wants to go to the mall._

2. **A:** What does she plan to do there? (buy new shoes)

   B: _____

3. **A:** What do you need to do? (study for my math test)

   B: _____

4. **A:** What did they decide to do? (stay home)

   B: _____

5. **A:** What did Daniel agree to do for the Community Festival? (sell tickets)

   B: _____

6. **A:** What did Elizabeth volunteer to do? (prepare sandwiches)

   B: _____

C **Circle the correct words**

1. I don't enjoy ((meeting)/ to meet) new people.

2. We didn't practice (playing / to play) the music before the meeting.

3. Dan doesn't plan (volunteering / to volunteer) next week.

4. He decided (working / to work) instead.

5. Manuela really dislikes (cleaning / to clean) up.

6. She hopes (helping / to help) another time.

D **Can the sentence be rewritten as verb + infinitive? If it can, rewrite the sentence. If it can't, write NCP (no change possible).**

1. I'll begin studying at 8:00. _I'll begin to study at 8:00_ .

2. We enjoy reading the newspaper. _____

3. Our neighbors like talking to us. _____

4. My cousin dislikes doing his homework. _____

5. He likes playing basketball. _____

6. We'll continue working on this tomorrow. _____

	Like	Dislike	Hope
Ed	travel	study	visit Australia
Marie	read	exercise	get a job in a library
Greg and Julie	play sports	cook	start a neighborhood volunteer group

E **Grammar Boost** **Look at the chart. Write sentences about the people.**

1. _Ed likes traveling. (Or Ed likes to travel.)_____

   _He dislikes studying._____

   _He hopes to visit Australia._____

2. _____

   _____

   _____

3. _____

   _____

   _____

LESSON 4 Everyday conversation

A Complete the conversation. Use the words in the box.

he do that	any idea why	can I help you	don't know what
I've lived	I think I can	think it's because	~~told me to come in~~

Omar: Hello. I called yesterday. The man on the phone ___told me to come in___.

1

Ms. Davies: How _____ today?

2

Omar: Well, I _____ to do. _____ in the

3   4

same apartment for ten years. Two weeks ago, the new landlord told us to

move. Now I don't have a place to live.

Ms. Davies: Do you have _____?

5

Omar: No. I pay my rent and follow the rules. I _____ he wants

6

to give the apartment to someone else. Can _____?

7

Ms. Davies: No, he can't. _____ help you.

8

B Read about Omar. Then write the reported requests.

Yesterday Omar talked to Ms. Davies about a problem with his landlord. Ms.
Davies told him to do some things.

1. Ms. Davies said, "Fill out this form."

    _____Ms. Davies told Omar to fill out this form_____.

2. Ms. Davies said, "Answer these questions."

    _____

3. Ms. Davies said, "Don't use a pencil."

    _____

C 🖩 Real-life math Study the voter poll. Answer the questions.

1. Do most people want a new library?

    _____

2. If half of the undecided people vote yes
   for the library, will the library be built?

    _____

3. How many undecided people must vote for the
   library for it to pass? _____

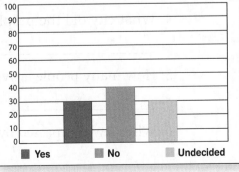

Voter Poll: Should We Build a New Library?

■ Yes   ■ No   ■ Undecided

A Read the article.

Civil Rights in Alabama

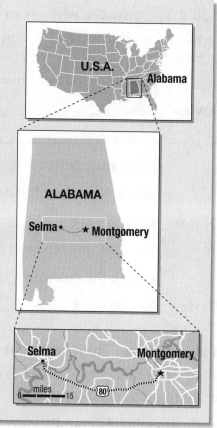

March 7, 1965
Many African Americans were not allowed to vote. Six hundred people started marching out of Selma, Alabama, to protest this discrimination. The marchers traveled only six blocks before they were beaten back[1] by state and local police. Many marchers were hurt in this push for civil rights.

March 9, 1965
Martin Luther King, Jr. led a second march to the Pettus Bridge to protest the beatings on March 7.

March 15, 1965
After hearing the reports of the violence in Alabama, U.S. President Lyndon B. Johnson signed the Voting Rights Act. This promised the right to vote to all American citizens.

March 21, 1965
After receiving court protection, 3,200 marchers began a third march from Selma to the state capitol in Montgomery.

March 25, 1965
After five days of marching (12 miles per day) and sleeping in fields, 25,000 marchers arrived in Montgomery.

August 15, 1965
Congress passed the Voting Rights Act.

[1] beaten back: fought against and forced to stop

B Write answers to the questions. Use complete sentences.

1. Where did the marches begin on March 7, 1965?

   The marches began in Selma, Alabama.

2. Who was the leader of the march to Pettus Bridge?

   _____

3. Who was the president of the U.S. in March 1965?

   _____

4. What city did the people march to?

   _____

5. How many people arrived there?

   _____

6. What law was passed by Congress because of the marches?

   _____

Write sentences and questions. Use the words in the boxes.

I	like	live	to	the city
you	enjoy	volunteer	in	the hospital
she/he	plan	go	at	the park
they		play		the school
		exercise		the senior center
				the health center
				Florida

Sentences

1. I enjoy volunteering at the senior center.

2. _____

3. _____

4. _____

5. _____

Questions

1. Did they plan to go to Florida?

2. _____

3. _____

4. _____

5. _____

Unit 1 Learning Together

Lesson 1 Vocabulary
page 2

A

make a study schedule–5
organize materials–6
search online–2
make an outline–3
(do) research–8
take a break–7
memorize words–4

B

2. d   5. a
3. e   6. c
4. b

Lesson 2 Real-life writing
page 3

A

2. to introduce
3. was nervous
4. to meet
5. talk about
6. first assignment
7. about ourselves
8. a presentation

B

2. T
3. T
4. F
5. F
6. T

Lesson 3 Grammar
page 4

A

2. finished his class
3. listen to the radio
4. wrote an essay
5. works
6. are studying in the library
7. is playing basketball
8. is reading a book

B

2. Alan took notes in class last night.
3. Hana did not memorize the new words last week.
4. We search the Internet every day.

5. They are not taking notes right now.
6. Our teacher helps us a lot every week.

page 5

C

2. f   5. a
3. d   6. c
4. e

D

Right now, Barbara and Carol are watching TV. They learn a lot by watching TV every day.

I like to use the Internet to find interesting ways to help me study. In our last class, the teacher asked us to bring in a newspaper article to the next class. Yesterday, I found an article about good study habits.

Did you go home to visit your family last week? Did you have a good time?

Lesson 4 Everyday conversation
page 6

A

2. so many choices
3. not sure
4. do you like
5. hard to say
6. worked in
7. studying economics
8. should think about

B

2. careful
3. quickly
4. well
5. easy

C

2. $144 \div 800 = .18$ or 18%
3. $96 \div 800 = .12$ or 12%
4. $400 \div 800 = .50$ or 50%

Lesson 5 Real-life reading
page 7

B

2. b   5. a
3. b   6. a
4. a

Another look
page 8

A

Present tense: use, speak, write, memorize
Past tense: used, made, went, studied

B

Adverbs: clearly, carefully, quickly

C

2. 40%
3. 75%
4. 80%
5. 20%
6. 10%
7. 60%
8. 50%
9. 70%
10. 30%

Unit 2 Ready for Fun

Lesson 1 Vocabulary
page 9

A

2. zoo
3. farmers' market
4. gym
5. nightclub
6. theater

B

2. a   5. f
3. d   6. c
4. b

Lesson 2 Real-life writing
page 10

A

2. Hi Oscar
3. are you
4. get together
5. at 5:00
6. to a concert
7. Think about
8. Talk to you soon

B

2. Sunday evening
3. 5:00
4. a concert
5. call

Lesson 3 Grammar
page 11

A
2. are going to go to the beach
3. is going to play sports
4. aren't going to sail
5. is going to swim in the ocean
6. isn't going to swim in the ocean

B
2. 's going to
3. will
4. 'll
5. is going to
6. 'll

page 12

C
2. will offer
3. will fix
4. will buy
5. will plan
6. will clean up

D
1. B: will
2. A: are, going to B: will
3. A: are, going to B: will
4. A: is going to B: will
5. A: Are, going to B: are going to be
6. A: are, going to B: will

Lesson 4 Everyday conversation
page 13

A
2. do you have in mind
3. up to you
4. I think I'd rather
5. I'll meet you
6. See you

B
2. A: Would, rather
   B: Answers will vary.
3. A: Would, rather
   B: Answers will vary.

C
1. $24
2. $26

Lesson 5 Real-life reading
page 14

B.
2. T   5. F
3. F   6. T
4. F

Another look
page 15

A.
Ivan: What are you going to do this afternoon?
Tina: We're going to see the new movie at the Town Theater. Do you want to come with us?
Ivan: No, thanks. We saw it last night. You'll love it.
Tina: I think I will. The newspaper says it's a great movie.
Ivan: We're going to have a party for Olga's sister tonight. Why don't you come by after the movie?
Tina: What time?
Ivan: The party is going to start at about 8:00. We'll be in the backyard. Walk around to the back of the house when you get there.
Tina: OK. We'll stop by after the movie.
Ivan: Great. I'll see you tonight.

B.
2. Plan
3. Prediction
4. Prediction
5. Plan
6. Plan
7. Promise
8. Promise
9. Promise

Unit 3 A Job to Do

Lesson 1 Vocabulary
page 16

A
2. It's $69.99.
3. It's $19.99.
4. It's $349.99.

B
2. photographer
3. graphic designer
4. office manager

C
2. a
3. d
4. c

Lesson 2 Real-life writing
page 17

A
2. Employee Policies
3. are arriving late
4. are taking 30-minute
5. are not cleaning their
6. must be at work by
7. may not eat or drink
8. Break times

B
2. b   5. b
3. b   6. a
4. a

Lesson 3 Grammar
page 18

A
2. not as heavy as
3. not as small as
4. more popular than
5. less expensive than
6. more reliable than

B
2. a
3. b
4. b

page 19

C
2. Phone Anywhere is the lightest.
3. Trans-Phone is the smallest.
4. Phone Anywhere is the least popular.
5. Trans-Phone is the most reliable.
6. Express Phone is the most popular.

D
2. larger
3. lower
4. friendliest
5. fastest
6. most complete

Lesson 4 Everyday conversation
page 20

A
2. is it
3. good worker
4. most creative person
5. You have to
6. won't have to tell

B
2. nicest
3. most patient
4. least efficient

C

2. History
3. 3.0

Lesson 5 Real-life reading
page 21

B

2. F
3. T
4. F
5. F
6. T

Another look
page 22

1. Leo is not as efficient as Rosa and Gloria. He is less efficient than Rosa and Gloria.
Leo is not as reliable as Rosa and Gloria. He is less reliable than Rosa and Gloria.
2. Rosa is not as organized as Gloria. Rosa is more organized than Leo.
Rosa is not as efficient as Gloria. Rosa is more efficient than Leo.
Rosa is not as reliable as Gloria. Rosa is more reliable than Leo.
3. Gloria is more organized than Leo and Rosa.
Gloria is more efficient than Leo and Rosa.
Gloria is more reliable than Leo and Rosa.

Unit 4 Good Work

Lesson 1 Vocabulary
page 23

A

Amy Kim
dress appropriately: yes
bring resume: no
leave cell phone on: yes
act nervous: no

Juan Perea
dress appropriately: no
bring resume: yes
leave cell phone on: no
act nervous: yes

B

2. d
3. f
4. a
5. c
6. e

Lesson 2 Real-life writing
page 24

A

2. of accounts manager
3. learning more about
4. organization and communication
5. 555-4114
6. Sincerely

B

2. b   4. a
3. a

Lesson 3 Grammar
page 25

A

2. have studied
3. have practiced
4. has had
5. has not fixed
6. have been
7. has not seen
8. have invited

B

2. since
3. since
4. for
5. for
6. for
7. since
8. for

page 26

C

2. has worked, since
3. has been, for
4. has not studied, since
5. has not written, since
6. has interviewed, since

D

2. don't live
3. live
4. feel
5. aren't

E

2. Emma and Paul have been married since 2002.
3. Paul hasn't studied English since last year.
4. They have lived in an apartment downtown for two months.
5. Paul has worked for Warwick Industries since December.

Lesson 4 Everyday conversation
page 27

A

2. I've been
3. for four
4. What makes you think
5. a good leader
6. Have you been
7. I'm a fast
8. can do it

B

2. He has worked
3. We have not done
4. She has gotten
5. She has been
6. The letter has not arrived
7. They have had
8. I have not talked

C

1. $172.00 per day
2. $860.00 per week

Lesson 5 Real-life reading
page 28

B

2. F
3. T
4. F
5. F
6. F
7. T
8. NI

Another Look
page 29

B

1. I've seen; He's trained; Nick has done; I've worked; We've made; I haven't had
2. Nick has been at Blue Skies music for eight years.
3. I've worked on two very interesting team projects since I started at Blue Skies.
We've made some big changes since then, and I think things are working better now.
4. I've, He's, He's, I've, We've, I haven't

Unit 5 Community Resources

Lesson 1 Vocabulary
page 30

A
2. f
3. d
4. c
5. e
6. a

B
2. open house
3. volunteer programs
4. pet adoption
5. wellness checkup

Lesson 2 Real-life writing
page 31

A
2. about a safety issue
3. are broken windows
4. discussed the problem
5. invite you to visit
6. can see the problem

B
2. a
3. b
4. d

Lesson 3 Grammar
page 32

A
2. Has Diana painted the apartment?
3. Has Kevin repaired the broken windows?
4. Have Leo and Chan been to the animal shelter?
5. Have you written a letter to the school board?
6. Have they taken a job-training class?
7. Have the children had a wellness checkup?
8. Have we discussed all the problems?

B
2. already
3. yet
4. ever
5. already
6. yet
7. ever
8. already

page 33

C
2. e
3. b
4. a
5. d

D
2. He has already painted the door.
3. He has already eaten lunch.
5. He hasn't bought more paint yet.
6. He hasn't fixed the broken window yet.

Lesson 4 Everyday conversation
page 34

A
2. so sorry
3. have you signed
4. What's it
5. We're asking
6. sounds like a great

B
2. go
3. had
4. volunteer
5. signed

C
2. 1980
3. 20

Lesson 5 Real-life reading
page 35

B
2. T
3. F
4. NI
5. T
6. NI

Another Look
page 36

A
Clean Up Now

B
2. She has volunteered to clean up trash.
3. She has planted trees in her community.
4. She has celebrated Earth Day.
6. She hasn't signed a petition.
7 She hasn't gone to a community meeting.
8. She hasn't reported a problem in her community.

Unit 6 What's Cooking?

Lesson 1 Vocabulary
page 37

A
boil–2
knife–6
chop–10
plate–3
fork–4
pour–7
stir–9
pot–5
bowl–8

B
2. grater
3. mixer
4. steamer
5. slicer
6. beater

Lesson 2 Real-life writing
page 38

A
2. away the groceries
3. and peeled it
4. stirred everything
5. secret ingredient
6. family secret

B
2. Cut up the bananas.
3. Put the bananas in a bowl with 2 eggs, 2 cups of flour, and 1 cup of sugar.
4. Stir everything together and pour into a pan.
5. Put the pan in the oven and cook for 45 minutes.
6. Take the bread out of the oven. Let cool and eat!

C
Rosa's Recipe for Banana Bread
    Take 4 bananas and peel them. Put the bananas in a bowl with 2 eggs, 2 cups of flour, and 1 cup of sugar. Stir everything together and pour into a pan. Put the pan in the oven and cook for 45 minutes. Take the bread out of the oven. Let cool and eat!

Lesson 3 Grammar
page 39

A
2. out
3. up

4. on
5. on
6. out

B

2. Can you figure them out?
3. Did you pick it up on your way home?
4. I didn't write them down.
5. I think we can turn it off now.
6. Did you turn it on?
7. I won't leave it out next time.
8. Did you put them in the bowl?

page 40

C

2. f   5. a
3. e   6. d
4. b

D

2. after
3. for
4. over
5. on

E

2. he looked for them.
3. we turned it off.
4. He figured them out.
5. she got over it.
6. they picked it up.

Lesson 4 Everyday conversation
page 41

A

2. have a question
3. chef doesn't use
4. cut down on
5. try them
6. are the best

B

2. yours, mine
3. Her, Ours
4. your
5. her, hers
6. My, yours

C

1. $1.90
2. $15.57

Lesson 5 Real-life reading
page 42

B

2. T
3. T
4. T

5. F
6. F

Another look
page 43

B

Possible answers:
1. put (them) in, write down, chop up, leave out, stir in
2. I put them in the pot and stir in my secret ingredient.
3. I always look for the freshest vegetables.
...I usually invite my friends to come over to my house for dinner.
4. my
5. mine

Unit 7 Money Wise

Lesson 1 Vocabulary
page 44

A

security guard–2
teller–4
loan officer–6
account services desk–5
open an account–3
apply for a loan–7
accounts manager–8

B

2. online banking
3. savings account
4. direct deposit

Lesson 2 Real-life writing
page 45

A

2. save money in
3. financial planning
4. share the cost
5. doesn't buy lunch
6. cheaper to bring
7. plans his shopping
8. reach his goal

B

2. F
3. NI
4. F
5. T
6. F
7. NI
8. T

Lesson 3 Grammar
page 46

A

2. e   5. f
3. a   6. c
4. b

B

3. doesn't fit
4. 'll look for
5. 'll buy
6. 's
7. use
8. 'll save

C

2. I will need $200
3. I will use a check
4. I will take pictures in the park.

page 47

D

2. if he saves money
3. if she has trouble with her car
4. if we find a good car
5. if you buy a new house

E

2. If they take a long vacation, Mike will travel to South America, and Luc will drive across the U.S.
3. If they win $1,000, Mike will buy a new bicycle, and Luc will open a savings account.
4. If the car doesn't work, Mike will ride his bicycle to work, and Luc will fix the car.
5. If they stay home this weekend, Mike will clean the house, and Luc will make dinner for his friends.
6. If there's a sale, Mike will not buy anything, and Luc will buy a cell phone.

Lesson 4 Everyday conversation
page 48

A

2. can I help you
3. that's impossible
4. talk to my supervisor
5. before we send
6. When you receive

B

2. after
3. After

4. If
5. after
6. if
C
7. $120
8. $125

Lesson 5 Real-life reading
page 49

B
2. a   5. b
3. b   6. a
4. b

Another look
page 50

2. If he buys a car, he will drive to California.
3. If he drives to California, he will need more money.
4. If he needs more money, he will need another job.
5. If he needs another job, he will look in the want ads.
6. If he looks in the want ads, he will get a better job.

Unit 8 Living Well

Lesson 1 Vocabulary
page 51

A
heart–3
stomach–4
bones–2
brain–5
lungs–7
muscles–8
intestines–6
B
2. e
3. d
4. a
5. c
6. f

Lesson 2 Real-life writing
page 52

A
2. Get in Shape
3. Lift weights.
4. Make medical and dental appointments.
5. See the dentist for cleanings.
6. Manage stress.

B
2. III
3. II
4. III
5. II
6. I
7. III
8. II

Lesson 3 Grammar
page 53

A

My cousin Julia is in great shape now, but she wasn't in the past. She <u>used to</u> be very sick and tired all the time. She <u>didn't use to</u> eat three meals a day. Sometimes she only ate once a day! She <u>used to</u> eat out often, but now she makes her own meals at home. She really enjoys cooking now. Julia didn't like sports, so she <u>didn't use to</u> exercise much. Now, she runs or jogs every morning. She's not tired any more. She <u>used to</u> look sad and worried, but now she's happy. She <u>used to</u> think that exercise was boring, but she doesn't now. She's healthy and happy. She feels great.

B
2. She used to watch TV all the time.
3. She didn't use to eat salads.
4. She used to eat lots of junk food.
5. She used to stay inside all day.
6. She didn't use to work outside.

C
2. he didn't use to take the subway.
3. my friends used to live near here.
4. they didn't use to play sports.
5. I used to take a walk every day.
6. I didn't use to get enough sleep.

page 54

D
2. did he use to practice
3. did Liz use to exercise
4. did you use to eat for lunch

5. did you use to go to the gym
6. did Katya use to eat fast food
7. did Joe use to study
8. How did Lara use to save money

E
2. rode, used to ride
3. drank, used to drink
4. didn't play, didn't use to play
5. went, used to go
6. didn't study, didn't use to study
7. didn't exercise, didn't use to exercise
8. ate, used to eat

Lesson 4 Everyday conversation
page 55

A
2. under a lot of
3. Have you been getting
4. I used to go
5. Why don't you
6. give it a try
B
2. has not been feeling
3. have been walking
4. have been talking
5. has been acting
C
1. 925 calories
2. 410 calories
3. Saturday
4. bike riding

Lesson 5 Real-life reading
page 56

B
2. T
3. T
4. NI
5. F
6. T
7. NI
8. F

Another look
page 57

A
Answers will vary.
2. I used to watch…
3. We used to play…
4. I used to…
5. I used to get up at…
6. I used to go to bed at night at…
7. I used to go on vacation to…

8. I used to... on vacations.
9. I used to play...
10. ...used to be my favorite singer.

B

Answers will vary.

Unit 9 Hit the Road

Lesson 1 Vocabulary
page 58

A

headlight–2
license plate–3
windshield–7
steering wheel–6
trunk–5
gas tank–8
tire–4
horn–10
bumper–9

B

2. f   5. d
3. a   6. e
4. b

Lesson 2 Real-life writing
page 59

A

2. you can see
3. and comfortable
4. we took a train trip
5. stayed there for
6. favorite part of
7. take my advice
8. be ready to
9. be sure to take

B

2. b
3. b
4. a

Lesson 3 Grammar
page 60

A

2. a   5. f
3. d   6. b
4. e

B

2. second, first
3. second, first
4. same
5. first, second
6. second, first

page 61

C

2. before

3. When
4. when
5. before

D

2. Sao changes the oil in his car before he takes a trip.
3. Irina will call after she picks up her car.
4. I hear the noise when I turn left.
5. Otto uses the turn signal before he makes a turn.

E

2. was
3. left
4. turns on
5. got out
6. hits

Lesson 4 Everyday conversation
page 62

A

2. two-year warranty
3. How much
4. It's going for
5. don't work
6. doesn't either
7. to my manager
8. work something out

B

2. and
3. too
4. but
5. either

C

1. $1,550.00
2. $1,367.65
3. Amarjit spent more on gas.

Lesson 5 Real-life reading
page 63

B

2. T
3. F
4. F
5. NI
6. T

Another look
page 64

1. After lunch, we continued for about another 4 hours.
2. We always take the car to our mechanic before we take a long car trip.
3. Nashville is not a large city, but there's a lot to do there.

4. Tomorrow we'll visit Centennial Park before we go home.
5. We took a bus tour of the city, and we went to the Country Music Hall of Fame, too.
6. It was late so we didn't have time to go into many stores, and we didn't have time to buy any souvenirs either.

Unit 10 Crime Doesn't Pay

Lesson 1 Vocabulary
page 65

A

2. walk alone
3. Walk in
4. Protect your wallet
5. commit a crime
6. report it
7. arrest a suspect

B

2. d   5. b
3. f   6. c
4. a

Lesson 2 Real-life writing
page 66

A

2. better lighting
3. a peephole
4. have a chain lock
5. to install a deadbolt lock
6. sleep better

B

2. a peephole
3. deadbolt lock, sleep better

Lesson 3 Grammar
page 67

A

Using our new system will make it more difficult for people to break in.
Entering a dark building at night doesn't have to be a problem.
Using our lighting system is easy.
Pushing just one button on your phone calls the police for you.
Reporting a crime is faster than ever before.
Staying safe is easy with Safety First.

B

2. Knowing
3. Walking
4. Installing
5. Carrying
6. Letting

C

2. G
3. P
4. P
5. G
6. P

page 68

D

2. Turning on
3. is making
4. am installing
5. Reporting
6. Protecting

E

2. isn't locking the door.
   Not locking the door
3. isn't watching other people.
   Not watching other people
4. isn't putting down her coffee.
   Not putting down her coffee

Lesson 4 Everyday conversation
page 69

A

2. like to report
3. what happened
4. First, they broke
5. after that
6. suddenly they ran
7. a complete report
8. Reporting this

B

2. Driving
3. lock
4. carry

C

1. People are most worried about someone hurting their child.
2. People are least worried about someone stealing their car.
3. 310 people are worried about someone breaking into their home.

Lesson 5 Real-life reading
page 70

B

1. animal control worker
2. fire inspector
3. driver's license examiner

Another Look
page 71

B

1. Walking alone at night can be scary.
Following some simple safety rules can protect everyone from crime.
Remember, watching the people around you can keep you safe.
2. A woman is walking home from the bank.
Her hands are shaking as she opens her front door.
3. What can you do to make sure you don't become a crime victim?
It's a good idea to walk with a friend.
It's important to find other people and a lighted area.

Unit 11 That's Life

Lesson 1 Vocabulary
page 72

A

2. e
3. f
4. a
5. d
6. b

B

2. married
3. Birth
4. born
5. Death
6. funeral

Lesson 2 Real-life writing
page 73

A

2. can't make it
3. out of town
4. a great party
5. for inviting us
6. excited to come
7. are looking forward
8. can bring anything

B

2. b
3. a
4. a

Lesson 3 Grammar
page 74

A

2. are sent
3. is decorated
4. is prepared
5. is performed
6. are taken

B

2. They're delivered at 4:45.
3. It's served at 5:00.
4. They're shown at 7:00.
5. It's closed at 9:00.

page 75

C

2. The flowers are delivered by Celia.
3. The pictures are taken by a professional photographer.
4. The music is performed by the Jones Family Jazz Band.
5. The wedding cakes are baked by Barry's Bake Shop.
6. The meal is prepared and served by the Green Meadows Restaurant.

D

2. is already made
3. is already decorated
4. are already wrapped
5. aren't washed yet
6. isn't prepared yet

Lesson 4 Everyday conversation
page 76

A

2. the bad
3. too bad
4. I'll be able to
5. That's great
6. Let's celebrate

B

1. B: wasn't able to find
2. A: won't be able to go
   B: wasn't able to attend
3. A: will be able to pass
   B: wasn't able to finish

C

1. 100 people
2. $2,150

Lesson 5 Real-life reading
page 77

B
2. T, no change
3. T, no change
4. F, If you buy a home, it belongs to you.
5. F, A down payment on a mortgage is usually larger than a security deposit.

Another look
page 78

B
2. The flowers are arranged.
3. The cake is baked.
4. The dress is made.
5. The tables are set.
6. The reception hall is decorated.
C
2. The waiters will be able to serve the food.
3. Gourmet Catering will be able to make the coffee.
4. Dan and Linda's family will be able to greet the guests.

Unit 12 Do the Right Thing

Lesson 1 Vocabulary
page 79

A
the right to a fair trial–2
freedom of speech–3
the right to vote–4
freedom of the press–5
freedom of peaceful assembly–6
B
2. f   5. a
3. e   6. d
4. b

Lesson 2 Real-life writing
page 80

A
2. work together to help
3. volunteered at
4. to vote for the
5. It's very important to
6. can make positive changes
B
2. T   5. T
3. NI   6. F
4. T

Lesson 3 Grammar
page 81

A
2. to start
3. to run
4. to serve
5. to announce
6. to clean up
B
2. She plans to buy some new shoes.
3. I need to study for my math test.
4. They decided to stay home.
5. He agreed to sell tickets.
6. She volunteered to prepare sandwiches.

page 82

C
2. playing
3. to volunteer
4. to work
5. cleaning
6. to help
D
2. No change possible.
3. Our neighbors like to talk to us.
4. No change possible
5. He likes to play basketball.
6. We'll continue to work on this tomorrow.
E
2. Marie likes to read. *or* Marie likes reading.
She dislikes exercising. She hopes to get a job in a library.
3. Greg and Julie like playing sports. *or* Greg and Julie like to play sports.
They dislike cooking. They hope to start a neighborhood volunteer group.

Lesson 4 Everyday conversation
page 83

A
2. can I help you
3. don't know what
4. I've lived
5. any idea why
6. think it's because
7. he do that
8. I think I can

B
2. Ms. Davies told Omar to answer these questions.
3. She told him not to use pencil.
C
1. No most people don't want a new library.
2. Yes, it will be built
3. Eleven of the undecided people must vote for it.

Lesson 5 Real-life reading
page 84

B
2. Martin Luther King Jr. was the leader.
3. Lyndon B. Johnson was the president of the U.S. in March 1965.
4. The people marched to Montgomery.
5. 25,000 people arrived there.
6. Congress passed the Voting Rights Act.

Another look
page 85

Answers will vary.